Native People of Wisconsin

◆ ◆ ◆

Patty Loew

Wisconsin Historical Society Press
Madison, Wisconsin

Published by the Wisconsin Historical Society Press

Photographs identified with PH, WHi, or WHS are from the Society's collections; address inquiries about such photos to the Visual Materials Archivist at the above address.

Publications of the Wisconsin Historical Society Press are available at quantity discounts for promotions, fund raising, and educational use. Write to the above address for more information.

Printed in the United States of America
Book design by Jill Bremigan

Front cover: three women with children—
Photo by A.C. Stone, WHi(X3)32712;
dancing boy—Photo by Verna L. deLeon;
doll in beaded cradleboard—Crandall
American Indian Doll Collection (H.H.
Bennett)

07 06 05 04 03   5 4 3 2 1

Library of Congress Cataloging-in-Publication Data
Loew, Patty.
    Native people of Wisconsin / Patty Loew.
       p. cm. — (The New Badger history series)
Summary: Introduces the twelve Indian nations that live
in Wisconsin, presenting tribal stories that incorporate
various ways Native people remember the past, and
emphasizing the value of oral tradition.
Includes bibliographical references and index.
    ISBN 0-87020-348-7 (text) — ISBN 0-87020-349-5 (teacher's guide)
1. Indians of North America—Wisconsin—History--Juvenile literature. 2. Indians of North America—Wisconsin—Social life and customs—Juvenile literature. [1. Indians of North America—Wisconsin. 2. Wisconsin—History.] I. Title. II. Series
    E78.W8L65 2003
    977.5004'97—dc21
                                                                                              2003011524
∞ The paper used in this publication meets the minimum requirements of the American National Standard for Information Sciences—Permanence of Paper for Printed Library Materials, ANSI Z39.48-1992

Other Titles in the New Badger History Series

(Includes classroom texts and teacher guides)

Series Editor: Bobbie Malone

Digging and Discovery: Wisconsin Archaeology

Learning from the Land: Wisconsin Land Use

Working with Water: Wisconsin Waterways

They Came to Wisconsin

Table of Contents

*Menominee Jerry Hawpetoss in
his pow wow outfit*

Photo by Lewis Koch for the Wisconsin Folk Museum
Woodland Indian Project, Courtesy of the UW-Madison
Folklore Program

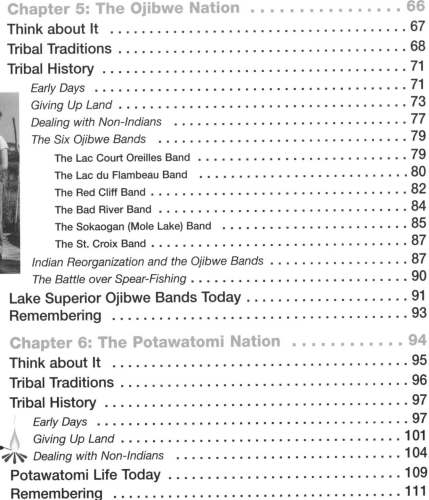

Introduction: First People of Wisconsin

On August 20, 1998, American Indian people danced in the homeland of their great-great grandparents. Today, it is known as Wisconsin. Before their ancestors were forced to leave, the land belonged to them. These people were the **Sauk** (sawk), **Mesquakie** (mes **kwaw** kee, also known as fox), the **Sioux** (soo), the **Potawatomi** (pah tah **wah** tuh me), from Kansas, **Kickapoo** (**kick** ah poo) from Oklahoma, and Nebraska **Winnebago** (wih neh **ba** go). They shared the land with the **Menominee** (meh **nah** mih nee), the **Ojibwe** (o **jib** way), the Potawatomi and the Ho-Chunk, who were related to the Nebraska Winnebago. Also dancing were the great-grandchildren and great-great grandchildren of the **Mohican** (mo **hee** can), **Oneida** (o **ny** dah), and Brothertown Indians, who arrived later, in the 1820s. For the first time in nearly 175 years, members of these Indian nations danced together. They celebrated their survival in the "New Dawn of Tradition Pow Wow."

As I waited with other traditional women dancers to enter the arena during the pow wow's grand entry, I was happy that people from these tribes had come back. But I felt a little sad too. The last time so many Wisconsin Native nations had been together was in 1825, at a grand **council** (**cown** suhl) in Prairie du Chien. Unhappily, the gathering had ended in a **treaty** (**tree** tee) that eventually led these Nations to giving up tribal lands to the government of the United States. The government also forced some Native people to move away.

Author Patty Loew at Indian Summer in Milwaukee

Photo courtesy of Patty Loew

council: A governing group ◆ **treaty:** An official, written agreement between nations

But some Native people decided to stay. Others found their way back to Wisconsin, or they moved here from other places and made it their home. *Native People of Wisconsin* is a book about the Native people who live in our state today.

Native People of Wisconsin introduces these Indian nations, but the book is not a complete study of the tribes in the state. It contains the short histories of the twelve Indian nations that live in Wisconsin: the Ho-Chunk, Menominee, Potawatomi, Oneida, Mohican, Brothertown, and six Bands of Ojibwe. Some Native people live on **reservations**. Some live in cities. Often Wisconsin Indian people celebrate their culture and traditions, which are different from those of non-Indians. But Native people also share many things in common with their non-Indian neighbors.

You will find several words used for the American Indian people you'll meet in this book: Native people, tribal people, tribe, and nation. The word *nation* appears in the book many times. Native people are legally citizens of *two* governments: the United States of America and their own Indian nation. That's because Indian governments existed before there was a United States. When the U.S. officials entered into treaties with Indian tribes, they recognized the tribes as **sovereign** (**sov** ren). Indian nations still possess **sovereignty** (**sov** ren tee) today, despite the fact that the U.S. Congress has attempted to place limits on it. If the relationship between Indian nations and the American government seems complicated, it is!

As a member of the Bad River Band of Lake Superior Ojibwe, I have not liked many of the history books about the Native Americans of this area. Many of the histories rely on the written words of early European visitors to the Great Lakes area. What these visitors learned is interesting, but not complete—and sometimes not even true. Native people have different of ways of telling history. For example, they use stories, songs, cave paintings, and objects that help keep the past alive. In this book, I have attempted to use many of these different ways of "telling" history.

Native people do not view everyday life the same way that non-Indians do. For example, they do not separate things that are **spiritual**—things that have to do with the soul and spirit—from those that have to do with the natural world. To Native people, everything that the Creator has given is **sacred** (**sa** cred), which means something deserving of respect. Thinking of our stories in a circle reflects that viewpoint.

reservations: Areas of land set aside by treaty for tribes to live on ◆ **sovereign:** As in "sovereign nation," independent; having the right to self-government ◆ **sovereignty:** Independence

This book has a few dates and timelines, but it tries to pay more attention to the way Native people think about history. That way, it introduces you to many of the stories, songs, dances, beadwork, and other ways Native people remember the past. In a history book like this one that contains *true* stories from the past, the words that real people have said or have written appear in quotation marks. This is to show that a real person actually said or wrote them.

Each chapter begins with a brief description of the past and present. The **Think about It** sections ask important and interesting questions about the chapter that will be answered as you read. Maps throughout the chapters will help you see the locations of tribal lands, and the movement and travels of the different nations. New vocabulary words are highlighted and their definitions appear at the bottom of the page. Other words and names appear in bold with pronunciation keys, so you'll know how they sound, even if you know their meanings. There's also a glossary at the end of the book where you can find all new words listed in alphabetical order.

As you read *Native People of Wisconsin,* you'll find that although the histories of the twelve Indian tribes in Wisconsin are different from one another, they share many things in common. You will also discover many things that these tribes have in common with non-Indians. Native peoples' stories are about values, about homes, about families, and about struggles to survive. Because we make our homes in Wisconsin, we just might find out something about ourselves in the stories—*our* stories—that help us understand more about our state's history.

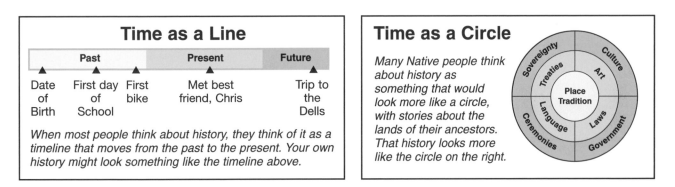

Time as a Line

	Past		Present	Future
▲	▲	▲	▲	▲
Date of Birth	First day of School	First bike	Met best friend, Chris	Trip to the Dells

When most people think about history, they think of it as a timeline that moves from the past to the present. Your own history might look something like the timeline above.

Time as a Circle

Many Native people think about history as something that would look more like a circle, with stories about the lands of their ancestors. That history looks more like the circle on the right.

Sovereignty · Culture · Treaties · Art · Place Tradition · Language · Laws · Ceremonies · Government

Chapter 1
Early History

◆ ◆ ◆

From the stories and songs passed down by each Nation, we have clues about how early Native peoples felt about the animals and plants that **sustained** them.

The story, "Fisher Goes to the Skyworld," shows how deeply the Ojibwe people respected and appreciated animals. In the story, four animals steal the sun and bring seasons to the earth. Mother Earth is dark and cold because the Sky People have captured the sun and all its warmth. Fisher, aided by his friends—Otter, Lynx, and Wolverine—digs a hole into the Skyworld and try to capture the sun. As the sun's rays escape, the earth begins to change. The snow melts, and the plants and trees appear. By the time the Sky People discover Fisher, he and his friends have dug a hole large enough for the sun to warm the earth for half the year. This story and others like it remind us that **ancient** (**ayn** chent) Native people viewed animals as helpers with their own spirits and purposes.

The songs and stories of Native people show that they thought of plants as helper spirits. In a Potawatomi story, the Creator "lifted up the whole world and dropped it in a lake," leaving only one young

sustained: Provided energy and strength and kept the people going ◆ **ancient:** Having existed a long time ago

woman. She was very much alone. Then, five strangers came to visit. The first visitor was tall and wore a green blanket that turned into tobacco leaves. The second was short and round. He rolled on the ground and became a pumpkin. The third and fourth visitors became beans and squash. The fifth was a handsome man whom the young woman married. After their wedding, the husband **revealed** himself to be the leader of the Corn Nation. Rain fell to bless them and many things grew. "The woman and the Corn Chief gave thanks to the Good Spirit," the Potawatomi remembered, "and taught their children how to pray and offer their thanks for corn, pumpkin, beans, squash, and tobacco."

Illustration by Joe Liles

The turtle has special significance for the Ojibwe and Oneida Nations.

Think about It

Who were the people who lived in Wisconsin long ago? How did they live? How did their lives and traditions change over time? How do we know about the lives of these early people?

Early Wisconsin people used spearpoints for hunting

revealed: Showed

Changes in Native Life

After the glaciers melted in Wisconsin, the land warmed, the lakes filled, and the rivers flowed. This gave the Native ancestors opportunities to learn new skills. During the next five thousand years, Native people taught themselves to shape copper into useful tools and other objects that they could trade with other communities. About one thousand years ago, some people began to grow crops, such as beans, squash, sunflower, and corn. They learned to select and plant the best seeds to ensure successful crops for the next year.

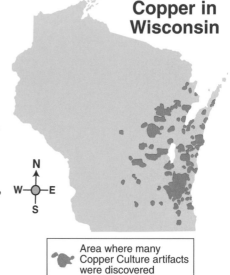

Copper in Wisconsin

N
W—E
S

Area where many Copper Culture artifacts were discovered

Map by Amelia Janes, Midwest Educational Graphics

Farming changed the lives of Native communities forever. Gardens of vegetables brought a very reliable and dependable food supply. But gardens needed care. As people stayed in one place longer to tend to their gardens, Wisconsin Indians began to build larger, more permanent villages. With more food, the number of people grew. Now that they lived together in communities, the people needed to develop ways to govern themselves so that everyone could get along peacefully. Groups of Native people also began trading more often with other groups. Native people also spent more time expressing themselves and their ideas in artistic ways. This can be seen in beautifully decorated pottery and in the amazing animal-shaped or **effigy** (**ef** fih jee) mounds that began to fill the landscape.

Native people shaped copper into tools to use and trade.

12

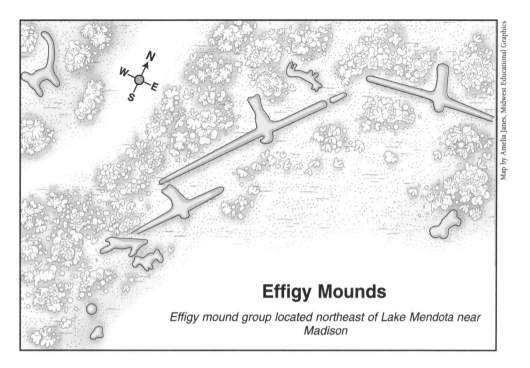

Effigy Mounds

Effigy mound group located northeast of Lake Mendota near Madison

Map by Amelia Janes, Midwest Educational Graphics

About 2,500 years ago, Native people began building round earthen mounds. Eventually, they shaped effigy mounds into the forms of humans and animals. Many mounds were of turtles, bears, and birds. Some of the mounds were huge! A bird effigy near the Wisconsin River in present-day Richland County had a wingspan of more than a quarter mile! That's longer than a city block.

Mound-builders had many reasons for pushing the earth into animal shapes. Sometimes these early Wisconsin Indians buried their dead in effigy mounds. Also it is likely that the mound-builders built effigy mounds near lakes and rivers because water is so important to life. Sometimes mounds were built in groups, and they often included panthers. Some Native people believe that the panthers represented underground spirits. The tails of these panther effigies seem to point to underground springs, which Native people believed were watery entrances to the underworld. This idea is found in the stories that Ho-Chunk people have passed down to their children.

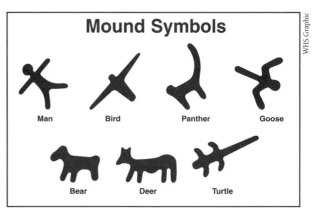
WHS Archives, WHi(X3)23678

Two-tailed animal mound

There are different ideas about what the animal symbols meant to the people who built the mounds. As you will read in the Ho-Chunk chapter, the effigy mounds may have had special meanings for different **clans**. Certainly, the effigy mounds had special meaning to those

WHS Graphic

Mound Symbols

Man   Bird   Panther   Goose

Bear   Deer   Turtle

who built them. These mounds represented sacred beliefs and served to mark the territory as belonging to their builders.

About a thousand years ago a group of Native people moved from the south into the Great Lakes area. They belonged to a powerful nation whose main city, **Cahokia** (cah **ho** kee ah) was near present-day St. Louis. At least 35,000 people lived in

clans: Groups of Native people with a common ancestor

Cahokia. This nation built large, flat-topped mounds, very different from the effigy mounds. This highly organized group of people traded goods with other people all across North America. In Wisconsin, this group built a village now known as **Aztalan** (**az** tuh lan), which is near present-day Lake Mills in Jefferson County. Those who built the village also constructed a high wooden wall around it. Inside this **stockade** , they built high platform mounds.

Location of Aztalan

Map by Amelia Janes,
Midwest Educational Graphics

Archaeologists (ar key **ol** o jists) find what people left behind and study how they lived. By digging up garbage and storage pits, archaeologists learned that the people of Aztalan grew lots of corn, beans, and squash. Their basic meat was **venison** , but they also ate duck, fish, and mussels. People living at Aztalan built their village along the west bank of the Crawfish River, which was full of fish and waterfowl. The soil was rich with natural minerals, making it excellent for farming. But despite this good location, the people abandoned their town after about ten generations. No one is sure why.

Platform mound at Aztalan

---

stockade: A series of high walls to keep out intruders ◆ **venison:** Deer

Woodland People

Long before the arrival of Europeans, many Indian people made present-day Wisconsin their home. While the Mesquakie and **Odawa** (o **dah** wuh, or Ottawa) people are no longer here, several other Indian Nations remain to this day. Many of these Native people were not related to one another, and did not speak the same language. Two groups, the Dakota Sioux and the Ho-Chunk, spoke **Siouan** (soo un) languages. The Dakota Sioux lived in the north and west, while the Ho-Chunk lived mainly in the central part of the state. The Dakota Sioux Nation no longer makes its home in Wisconsin, but the Ho-Chunk Nation is still here.

Evidence of Woodland Cultures Today

Map by Amelia Janes, Midwest Educational Graphics

The Menominee, Ojibwe, and Potawatomi spoke **Algonquian** (al **gon** kwin) languages and lived in the northeast, central, and southern sections of the state. As you might expect, all Siouan and Algonquian-speaking tribes shared many things in common because they lived in similar woodland environments. Where were the other Woodland peoples—the Oneida, the Mohican Nation, Stockbridge-Munsee Band, and Brothertown—that are now in Wisconsin? The Mohican Nation,

Stockbridge-Munsee Band and Brothertown Indians have been in Wisconsin since the 1820s. The Mohican Nation, Stockbridge-Munsee Band and the Brothertown Indians speak Algonquian languages, but the Oneida speak **Iroquoian** (ear o **qwoy** yun). The Stockbridge people, the Delaware Munsee, and the Brothertown come from homelands in the northeast. You'll learn more about these Nations as you continue reading.

Wisconsin's Native people lived in wigwams made from bent tree saplings covered with bark. They ate similar foods. They hunted deer, rabbit, and waterfowl. They fished for sturgeon, pike, lake trout, and catfish. They gathered nuts, wild rice, berries, edible plants, sap from maple trees and shellfish. They also planted corn, beans, squash, tobacco, and sunflowers. Communities farther north, such as the Ojibwe, had shorter growing seasons, so they farmed less than the Ho-Chunk and Menominee. Because they did more

Waswagoning (wahs wah goh ning) is a recreated Ojibwe village at Lac du Flambeau.

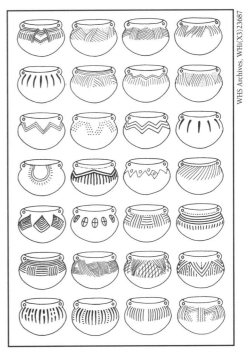

Woodland people decorated their pots in many ways.

hunting, trapping, and sugaring, the Ojibwe lived in smaller groups, or **bands**, that could travel together easily from one seasonal location to another. The Ho-Chunk and Menominee tended to live in larger villages.

Clans

Each Nation organized itself into clans. The Menominee and the Ho-Chunk divided their clans into two groups, with one representing the earth, and the other representing the sky. Among the Menominee, peace chiefs came from the earth clans, which included the Bear Clan. The sky clans, such as the Eagle, produced the war chiefs. In Ho-Chunk culture, the roles of the clans were reversed: Sky Clan chiefs were leaders during times of peace; earth clan chiefs led their communities in times of war.

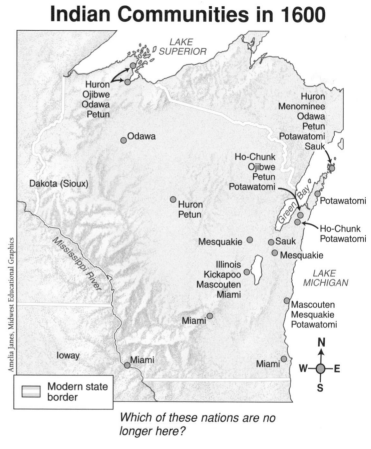

Indian Communities in 1600

Amelia Janes, Midwest Educational Graphics

Which of these nations are no longer here?

Clan leaders, or chiefs, did not "rule" in the manner of European kings or queens.

They led by the **consent** (cun **sent**) of the people, which meant they had to get tribal members to agree with them. Nations expected their leaders to be generous and to put the interests of the community above their own. They especially liked leaders who were good speakers and were clever in dealing with other groups. Speaking well and being clever were useful skills in making treaties and forming **alliances** (a **li** un ses).

Different Paths to the Past

Passing down stories by telling them over and over without writing them down is known as **oral tradition**. About a thousand years ago, an artist rubbed smooth the walls of a rock shelter that was hidden in a wooded valley in southwestern Wisconsin. The artist carefully made red, black, and blue-gray paints and painted turtles, thunderbirds, and a hero who wore human heads as earrings. This rock-art painter was as much a historian as he was an artist. These images tell the story of Red Horn,

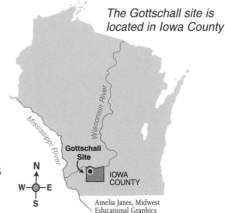

The Gottschall site is located in Iowa County

Amelia Janes, Midwest Educational Graphics

an ancient Ho-Chunk hero. Ho-Chunk people have been telling Red Horn's story to their children and to their children's children ever since, and this is a good example of oral tradition.

The rock shelter itself, known today as the **Gottschall** (**got** shawl) site, is located in present day Iowa County. This shelter is just one of more than a hundred rock art sites in Wisconsin.

alliances: Friendly agreements between groups

MORE ABOUT ROCK ART

Ancient rock art includes all images that were carved or painted on stone walls. No one knows exactly why Native people created this art, but archaeologists believe that they did it to teach the young or to remember the dead. The images, preserved in stone, also may have helped people remember important events or **ceremonies** (**ser** uh mo neez).

Rock art, effigy mounds, and oral tradition can help us learn about the Native cultures that began in Wisconsin long before Europeans arrived. Stone tools, pottery, and other objects can also provide us with more information. Archaeologists believe that humans have lived in the Great Lakes region for at least twelve thousand years. According to the ancient stories of most Indian Nations in Wisconsin, their people have been here "from the beginning of time."

Photo by Charles Brown

This image of a thunderbird was found at Twin Bluffs in Juneau county.

ceremonies: Formal actions, words, or songs that mark an important occasion, such as a wedding or funeral

Remembering

We can learn about the early history of the ancestors of Native people in Wisconsin by doing different kinds of research. We study the things left from the past in the same way archaeologists do. Or we can learn from oral tradition by listening to stories from the past, which is the way Native people have always done. Both kinds of research may represent a new way for you to learn about the past. If archaeologists had not worked with present-day Ho-Chunk **Elders,** the Red Horn painting at the Gottschall rock shelter might have remained a complete mystery. The ancient songs, stories, and art of Native people are filled with wisdom about life. In order to understand the people, places, events, and the ideas that shaped their lives, we must not only *read* history, but we must *visit with it* and *listen to* those who can share it with us.

Jim Frechette carved this Menominee sculpture.

Chapter 2

European Arrivals

◆ ◆ ◆

In the summer of 1634, the Ho-Chunk, Menominee, and Potawatomi saw a strange sight near present-day Green Bay. It was a light-skinned visitor carrying gifts and metal objects. The Ho-Chunk described the objects as "thunder sticks." The visitor was **Jean Nicolet** (jhan nik oh **lay**), a French trader. The governor of New France in North America sent Nicolet to look for a Northwest Passage to China. He also wanted Nicolet to try to stop the fighting between the Ho-Chunk and the Odawa Nations.

Jean Nicolet, French fur trader

The fighting between these tribes was making it hard for the French to expand their fur trade into the western Great Lakes region. Do you know what Nicolet's "thunder sticks" were? Guns! And guns would forever change life for the Wisconsin Indian Nations.

Because some American Indian **prophecies** (**prof** eh seez) told of the arrival of "light-skinned, hairy ones," the Ho-Chunk leaders welcomed Nicolet to their village of Red Banks. Long before they ever saw Nicolet, the Ho-Chunk had probably heard that a pale-skinned people had arrived in the east. Such amazing news probably traveled

prophecies: Predictions about future events

very quickly through the Native trade networks that reached across North America. But "quickly" in those days meant weeks or months. Today, radio, television, and the Internet can tell us instantly about different people in countries all over the world. But when Nicolet arrived in Wisconsin nearly four hundred years ago, these inventions did not exist.

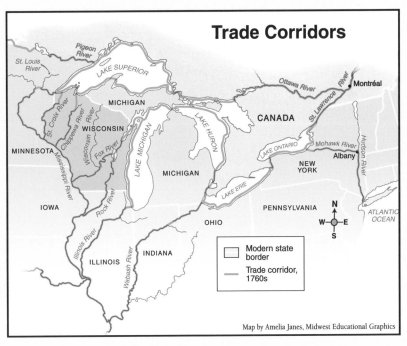

Trade Corridors

Modern state border

Trade corridor, 1760s

Map by Amelia Janes, Midwest Educational Graphics

Think about It

What do you think Native peoples thought and felt the first time they saw a European?

Other than guns, what did Europeans bring that changed life for Wisconsin Indian Nations? How did everyday life for *all* American Indian people change after the arrival of Europeans?

Native People Moving West

Even before they actually came to Wisconsin, Europeans had begun to change the lives of the American Indians in the region. Farther east, the French and their Algonquian-speaking **allies** (al leyes) were at war with the the Dutch and their Five Nations allies. **Refugee** (ref yoo jee) nations escaping the violence moved west into the lands of the Ho-Chunk and Menominee. These refugee nations included the Sauk, **Mascouten** (mas **coo** ten), Potawatomi, and Kickapoo. They moved west and north after leaving the southern edge of Lake Michigan. The Ojibwe, Odawa, and Mesquakie were among those who settled along the northern boundaries of Ho-Chunk and Menominee territory. When these new people arrived, they pushed the Ho-Chunk south toward their enemies, a powerful group of American Indians from Illinois.

The **tension** (**ten** shun) between the Odawa and the Ho-Chunk had grown especially fierce. Nicolet

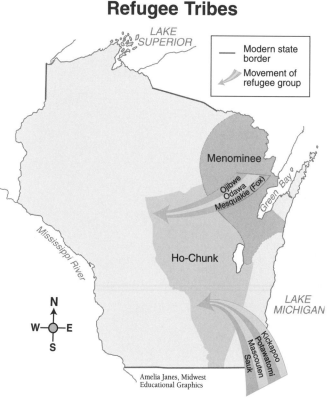

Refugee Tribes

LAKE SUPERIOR

| | Modern state border |
| | Movement of refugee group |

Menominee

Ojibwe
Odawa
Mesquakie (Fox)

Green Bay

Ho-Chunk

Mississippi River

LAKE MICHIGAN

Kickapoo
Potawatomi
Mascouten
Sauk

N
W—◆—E
S

Amelia Janes, Midwest
Educational Graphics

allies: Friends, especially during wartime ◆ **refugee:** People who are forced by war or disaster to leave their homes ◆ **tension:** Fear and worry

hoped to make it safe for his Indian allies to trade fur. Within a year of his arrival, however, the Ho-Chunk and Menominee people were at war with the refugee Nations. During the next few years, the Mesquakie people became a continuing threat to the Ho-Chunk.

As the fighting grew worse, the Illinois tribes nearly destroyed the Ho-Chunk in the 1640s. When French fur trader Nicholas **Perrot** (puh **roh**) and **Jesuit** (**jehz** wit) priest Claude-Jean **Allouez** (ahl oh **way**) arrived at Green Bay, they found only five hundred Ho-Chunk survivors in a village ruined by starvation and disease. More than ninety percent of the Ho-Chunk people had died. The surviving Ho-Chunk members wanted to stay together as a community, so they married their sons and daughters to members of other nations. They believed that this was the only way to rebuild their nation.

The Menominee people were strong Ho-Chunk allies. But they had suffered from battles with the refugee Nations, too. With so many more people and constant warfare, natural resources were soon **depleted** (de **plee** ted). The most important of these resources were edible plants and game animals.

Tribes quarreled over fishing grounds. Sometimes, these quarrels turned into wars as Native people fought over resources that were disappearing quickly. But the warfare only made all tribes weaker.

confederacy: groups (like the Five Nations) that band together for a common purpose ◆ depleted: Used up

The French Fur Trade

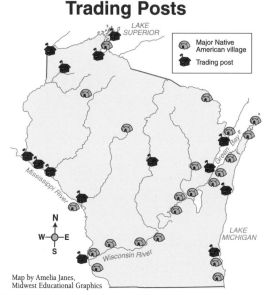

By 1649, the French fur trade was in trouble. The Huron people had helped to build the trade between the Great Lakes tribes and the French. Then the Huron enemies, the Five Nations, almost completely destroyed them. Without the help of the Huron people, the Great Lakes tribes had to take their furs all the way to Montreal, which was hundreds of miles to the east. The canoe trip was dangerous because it took Great Lakes tribes into areas controlled by the hostile Five Nations. Only the Ojibwe, Odawa, and Potawatomi people, known as the **Anishinaabe** (ah nih shih **nah** bay), attempted this difficult journey. They did it by organizing into large groups of canoes that could fight their way past enemy warriors.

Map by Amelia Janes, Midwest Educational Graphics

In 1659, two French traders paddled into western Lake Superior and offered to trade with the Great Lakes tribes. After a year of trading, the French traders returned to Quebec, the capital of New France (now Canada). The traders carried a large cargo of furs and other trade items. However, they did not have a **license** (**li** suhnts) to trade there, so the French government took away their cargo. Despite this, the news spread of good trading in the Great

German silver bangle
WHS Museum Collection

license: Permission or approval from a government ◆ **Anishinaabe:** The ancient name for a group formed by the Ojibwe, Odawa, and Potawatomi tribes

Lakes region. Soon, more and more unlicensed traders arrived.

The tribes welcomed these ***coureurs de bois*** (coo **rer** deh bwah) or "woods runners." Indian communities could now trade closer to home, which kept them away from the territory of the Five Nations. For the French government, however, the coureurs de bois were a problem. They did not pay **royalties** to the Crown. But a more serious problem arose. The uncontrolled trading created more furs than were needed. Too many furs made the prices lower! When the king of France officially forbade the tribes to trade with the coureurs de bois, Indian traders simply ignored the order.

Great Lakes

Map by Amelia Janes, Midwest Educational Graphics

The French responded by closing their western forts and moving their official traders back east to big trading centers such as Detroit. The French wanted their American Indian trading partners to move closer to these centers. And some of the refugee tribes did move east and resettle near Detroit. When they left, the Menominee and Ho-Chunk were able to return to the lands where they had lived when the Europeans first arrived.

royalties: Payments, sometimes in the form of taxes

The British Arrival

In the 1740s, British traders began moving westward into the Ohio River Valley. This made life for Native people more complicated. With conflicts between American Indians increasing, they had a hard time trying to decide which European group— the French or the British—would make the better ally. As more and more British people arrived, the French began building or reopening old forts, including one at Green Bay and another at

Location of Fort Michilimackinac
Amelia Janes, Midwest Educational Graphics

Michilimackinac (mish lih **mak** ih naw). This fort on present-day **Mackinac** (**mak** ih naw) Island became a main trading fort for the Great Lakes tribes.

The Indian Nations of the Great Lakes reacted differently to the arrival of the British than they had to the French. The Anishinaabe, who had become friends with the French, were uneasy. But the Menominee and Ho-Chunk were hopeful that life might be better. They had disliked the French traders and the special treatment that favored the Anishinaabe.

In the beginning, English trade practices were very different from those of the French. The French had given many gifts to their Indian partners, but the British gave no presents. The commander of the British army in North America believed that gift-giving—an important custom in tribal culture—was just **bribery** (**bri** buh ree). The French had supplied Native trading partners with ammunition for hunting and food during harsh winters. But a British commander chose not to follow this custom.

bribery: Gifts offered to people in exchange for favors

He also insisted that all trading be done inside the fort. He did this to control the alcohol, weapons, and ammunition that were traded, but the tribal communities resented this treatment. When Pontiac, the son of an Odawa chief and an Ojibwe mother, organized a huge military effort to get rid of the British, every tribe except the Menominee and Ho-Chunk Nations offered their support.

Trying to Get Rid of the British

In April 1763, Pontiac organized a war council attended by four hundred chiefs and warriors. In early June, Ojibwe, Potawatomi, Sauk, and Mesquakie warriors attacked fourteen British forts and eventually managed to capture most of them, including Fort Michilimackinac and Fort Edward Augustus in Green Bay. This **rebellion** (re **bel** yun) failed to remove the British permanently. But it did force the British to limit non-Indian settlements on Indian lands. Many colonists ignored this law and kept moving west.

In the late 1700s, the British changed the way they traded. The new practices improved life for Native people, and British trade grew. The British once again started giving gifts and selling guns and ammunition to the tribes. American Indians became loyal to the British. When the American colonists fought against the British in the late 1700s and early 1800s, most of the Wisconsin tribes fought on the side of the British.

German silver pin
WHS Museum collection

---

rebellion: Armed fight against a government

FRENCH NAMES

Today, hundreds of tribal members carry the names of early French traders, such as **Grignon** (**gree** noh), **Corbine** (**cor** bin), **Denomie** (**den** oh mee), and **Cadotte** (kah **dot**). Together, the French and their American Indian allies created what came to be called a "Middle Ground." This new way of life borrowed and blended parts of both French and American Indian traditions.

Brass Kettle
Illustration by Pheobe Hefko

When the French first arrived in the Great Lakes region, they were interested mainly in trade. They saw the Great Lakes tribes as good trading partners. Some French trading families even sent their sons to live in Indian communities, so they could learn the language, become friends, and even marry into Native families. The ***voyageurs,*** (voy uh **jurz**) were the French-Canadian traders who canoed along the waterways of the Great Lakes and adopted Native foods, medicines, dress, and customs. Many of these traders married American Indian women and became part of their communities.

The languages, trade goods, and culture of the Europeans greatly changed the lives of all Great Lakes Native people. At first, the changes seemed good. European metal hoes, axes, and tools helped clear the land. The Ho-Chunk and Menominee people became better farmers. Copper kettles, knives, and other utensils made many other chores much easier. Guns and traps helped the Potawatomi and Ojibwe tribes became better hunters.

Because these European goods made life easier, many Native communities wanted to be part of the fur trade. But, as time went by, the fur trade harmed the way they lived. Native people grew poorer as the fur trade depleted natural resources.

Dependence upon trade goods also changed the way Native people lived. When Indian hunters could no longer find fur-bearing animals in their own territories, they would move into the hunting grounds of neighboring tribes. Because of this, tribes then disagreed and sometimes fought one another. Even the way Indian communities were organized changed to meet the demands of hunting. The Ho-Chunk Nation and others had lived in larger villages before the Europeans arrived. Now Wisconsin's Native people separated into smaller bands. Smaller bands could help them track game and harvest **pelts** better and faster than before.

Since male hunters were gone for longer and longer periods of time, women's roles changed. Women gained independence as they took on more responsibilities. They built and repaired their lodges. They gathered firewood, hunted game animals, and did much more heavy work than they were used to. With the men gone, women took over the responsibility of providing all the food for their families. The women quickly began to rely on the crops for their family's survival. When the male hunters were gone from home for so long, life was harder for everybody.

Also, the Europeans wanted a single leader with whom to do business. But many tribes did not have one leader; they were governed by group consent. With no single person to speak for American Indian communities, the French sometimes simply picked their own Indian "chiefs." By giving these individuals special attention and trade goods, the non-Indians created, in the words of one nineteenth-century Ojibwe historian, "jealousies and heart-burnings." Bad feelings and resentments between tribal members further weakened the tribes.

pelts: Animal furs that are dried, and sometimes sewed, for trade

31

Christianity also changed Native cultures. In the 1660s, Jesuit **missionaries** (**mish** shun air eez) came to the western Lake Superior area. The Christian promise of heaven looked good to some of the Native people after the disease, warfare, and the great changes of the late 1600s. Native peoples saw that the Jesuits often stayed healthy while diseases were destroying Native communities. Some thought that the Christian God would protect them, and the Jesuits **converted** these Native people to Catholicism.

In 1673, Missionary Jacques Marquette and fur trader Louis Jolliet were the first Europeans to travel from Green Bay to the Mississippi River.

Jesuit Ring
Illustration by Phoebe Hefko

But the Ojibwe people had mixed feelings about the **Muk-a-day-i-ko-na-yayg** (muck a **day** ee ko nah yayg), or "Black Coats," as they called the Jesuits. At times the Ojibwe considered the priests to be helpful. But, for the most part, the Ojibwe felt that these Europeans were less respectful of Indian ways than the French traders had been. For example, the Jesuits turned some tribal members away from the **Midewiwin** (mih **day** wih win), the traditional Medicine Lodge religion. The Jesuits also wanted newly converted Indians to turn away from those who continued to follow the Midewiwin way.

converted: Changing the spiritual beliefs of a group or individuals ◆ **missionaries:** religious people who try to persuade others to become Christian

Remembering

The arrival of Europeans into North America changed the lives of Native people forever.

Refugee tribes fleeing the Europeans in the northeast made life difficult for other Native people even *before* Nicolet reached Wisconsin. Also, conflicts among Native people grew as they shifted loyalties from one European group to another. When the fur trade brought new trade goods and new cultures (languages, customs, and religions), life seemed easier. But as natural resources were depleted, life got harder. Many of the European trade practices treated Wisconsin Indian people unequally and unfairly. As more Europeans and European-Americans arrived in the 1800s, life for Native people only got worse.

Chapter 3

The Menominee Nation

♦ ♦ ♦

When many people think of the Menominee people, they think of the forest. The Menominee people believe that their history and traditions began with the white pines and sugar maples of the western Great Lakes. The forest has always given the tribe everything it needed to live, and the forest continues to sustain the Menominee way of life to this day. As a present-day member of the Menominee Nation has said, "We are the forest." Yet, outsiders throughout Menominee history have threatened their forest and its resources. The struggle to preserve their forest nearly cost the Menominee people their land and their **identity** (eye **den** tih tee) as an Indian people.

WHS Archives, WHi(X3)26181

The forest is important to the Menominee people.

identity: Who you are

Think about It

Why did the Menominee Nation have to fight outsiders to protect their land? In what ways did they have to struggle? What happened that nearly cost the nation its identity? What are the Menominee people doing to protect their interests today?

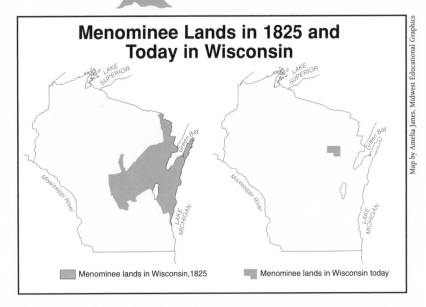

Menominee Lands in 1825 and Today in Wisconsin

Menominee lands in Wisconsin, 1825

Menominee lands in Wisconsin today

Map by Amelia Janes, Midwest Educational Graphics

You will encounter many new words in this chapter, more than in any other in the book. Learning these challenging words will help you to better understand this chapter—and the entire story of *Native People of Wisconsin*.

Tribal Tradition

The Menominee say they are **Kiash Matchitiwuk** (kee ahsh mah che te wuck), which means the "Ancient Ones." Their oral tradition tells us that the Menominee have always lived in this region. Their stories describe how the tribe was created at the mouth of the Menominee River, just sixty miles from the present-day Menominee reservation. According to this history, the Creator transformed a bear into a human. The bear found that he was alone, and he called to an eagle. When the eagle came down, it too became a human. The Creator then gave them "the river, the fish, the wild rice, and the sugar trees," and told them that they would always have these.

From this beginning, the bear and eagle adopted other animals. These became clans of the tribe. Five clans began at the mouth of the Menominee River. These clans were the Bear, Eagle, Wolf, Moose, and Crane Clans. They helped organize the way of life within the tribe. Each clan was a source of knowledge, and each had special duties. For example, members of the Bear Clan were speakers and keepers of the law. The Crane Clan was known for its skills in art and how to build things.

As with other Woodland tribes, Menominee life followed the seasons. In the summer, there was plenty of food. People fished, hunted, and collected roots, berries, and nuts. They also planted gardens. In late summer, the Menominee harvested their wild rice. During the fall and long winter months, the people lived off of the meat brought in by hunters and the food they had stored during the

Sturgeon
Illustration by Brian Strassburg

summer. In the spring, when the days were warm, and nights were freezing, the people collected and processed maple sugar. Then they anxiously waited for the return of the sturgeon. After months of extremely cold nights and dark days, food supplies were at their lowest. The Menominee eagerly celebrated the annual return of the sturgeon up the Wolf River. Finally, food would be plentiful again.

Menominee Sculptures by Artist Jim Frechette

Bear winnowing wild rice

Golden Eagle

Marten

Menominee sculptor Jim Frechette at work

Tribal History

Early Days

After the French arrived in the 1600s, the Menominee faced great and stressful changes. They experienced warfare, disease, and confusion when new people, both Indian and non-Indian, moved into Menominee territory from the east. Menominee life changed as the tribe relied more upon European trade goods. Metal pots took the place of clay ones. Guns and knives replaced stone tools. To get these goods, men had to spend more and more time hunting for furs and were forced to stay farther and farther from their homes. The old ways of doing things were changing.

Fort Michilimackinac

The American Revolution brought even more changes for the Menominee people. Tribal members provided the British with canoes, furs, and other supplies. Like most Indian tribes in the Great Lakes area, they joined the British in battles against the Americans. Even though the Americans eventually won the war, few American traders came into Menominee country at this time. The British stayed.

Events taking place in the east gradually drew the Menominee into another war between the Americans and the British. This war was called the War of 1812. In July of that year, about forty Menominee warriors, a group of Ho-Chunk and Sioux, a British officer, and a trader, took Fort Michilimackinac without firing a shot. Among the Menominee warriors was a seventeen-year-old named Oshkosh. When the war ended,

Oshkosh became the leader of the Bear Clan, with the guidance of the great Menominee war chief Tomah. This happened just as the Menominee began facing important decisions about their land. Do these names sound familiar? Did you know that the cities of Oshkosh and Tomah were named for these important Menominee leaders? Many place names in Wisconsin are clues to our history!

The Wolf River flows through the Menominee Reservation.

Giving Up Land

In the 1820s, groups of Christian Indians from New York—the Oneida, Stockbridge, and Brothertown—were looking for land farther west. Non-Indian settlers had been pushing these tribes from their eastern homelands, so the tribes asked the Menominee and Ho-Chunk Nations to share their land. Under pressure from the U.S. government, the Menominee and Ho-Chunk agreed to share a narrow strip of land along the Fox River north of Lake Winnebago. At a second meeting, non-Indian **negotiators** (nih **go** shee ay terz) managed to get the size of the land increased. This territory now included the "whole of the Menominee country East and North of Winnebago Lake."

The Menominee thought they were agreeing to *share* land with the New York Indians. Instead, the non-Indian negotiators were setting it up as a land **cession** (**seh** shun). When the Oneida, Mohican, and Brothertown Indians arrived in the 1820s, the Menominee were worried about what might happen to their land. In 1832, after years of government pressure, Menominee representatives signed a treaty to **cede** (seed)

negotiators: People who help in making agreements ◆ **cession:** The act of giving up one nation's land to another
cede: To give up land to another

39

Photo courtesy of Great Lakes Intertribal Council

three million acres. The area included 500,000 acres "for the benefit of the New York Indians." In exchange, the Menominee were promised $146,500 over the next twelve years.

Chief Oshkosh

The pressure to give up more land did not end with this treaty. The U.S. government insisted that non-Indian settlers should have the land for farming. In 1836, the Menominee were forced to give up the eastern half of their remaining territory. In 1848 they were forced to give up the remaining western half. When Wisconsin became a state, the president of the United Sates ordered the Menominee to leave their homes and move to a small reservation in the Crow Wing River area of Minnesota. A group of Menominee clan leaders, including Oshkosh, visited this Minnesota land. When they returned, they told tribal members that Crow Wing was not good for the Menominee people. Oshkosh announced that "the poorest region in Wisconsin was better than the Crow Wing." He also said that the constant fighting between the Dakota and Ojibwe people in the area would threaten the lives of his people.

Oshkosh and other leaders went to Washington D.C. They met with the president. Many Indian nations east of the Mississippi River were being removed to land west of the Mississippi. But the Menominee were able to persuade the President to temporarily stop the removal order. Over the next several years, the Menominee council delayed moving. The tribe's **persistence** (pur **sis** tentz) paid off. In the Treaty of 1854, the Menominee were able to reserve 276,000 acres of thick forest

persistence: Refusing to give up on what you want to accomplish

along the Wolf and Oconto Rivers as a permanent home. They chose this land so that they could be close to the sturgeon migrating up the Wolf River.

Dealing with Non-Indians

After the Menominee land decision was settled, the tribe bought a sawmill that a non-Indian had set up on their land without permission. Then, the tribe began cutting small amounts of timber. Oral tradition describes how the Menominee were supposed to log their land. Their Elders advised them to begin cutting only the **mature** (mut **chur**) trees. The loggers were to begin in the east and work west. When they reached the western boundaries of the reservation, the trees in the east would then be ready for them to harvest.

Logging on the Menominee Reservation about 100 years ago. Have you seen trees this large in Wisconsin?

Sawmill at Neopit on the Menominee Reservation, 1950

WHS Archives, WHi(X3)33623

WHS Archives, WHi(X3)9633

mature: Fully grown or developed

The success of their sawmill allowed the Menominee to keep their tribal lands. In the late 1880s, other Wisconsin tribes had their lands **allotted** (uh **lah** ted). Under the General Allotment Act of 1887, tribal land was divided and given to individual tribal members instead of belonging to the whole tribe. Dividing up the land was part of an effort by the U.S. government to force American Indians to live more like non-Indians. The government hoped that Indians would become self-sufficient farmers, living on their own parcels of land instead of living on lands held by the tribe. The Menominee people voted against allotment.

But tribal members could not escape the government's other efforts to **assimilate** (ah **sih** muh late) them, or to make them live like non-Indians. The government controlled the education of Indian children. For a while there was actually a rule that stated, "Indian parents have no right to select which school their children shall attend." What do you think your parents would say if the government decided where you should go to school and sent you away?

WHS Archives, WHi(X3)52672

Indian boarding school at Keshena. Can you guess the age of some of these students?

allotted: To share part of something ◆ **assimilate:** To make similar or to blend cultures and customs with another

Some Menominee children were sent to government boarding schools in Wisconsin, mainly to Lac du Flambeau, Tomah, and Hayward. Some were sent as far away as South Dakota and Pennsylvania. Other children remained on the reservation and attended St. Joseph's Catholic School or the government boarding school in Keshena. In some schools, Menominee children were not allowed to speak their native language or to take part in Menominee customs. How would you feel if people who had a different culture and different customs forced you to live they way they lived? What if you were punished every time you spoke your native language?

In the early 1900s, some members of the Menominee Nation continued to live off what they could hunt, fish, and gather. Many other tribal members found jobs in the timber industry. By 1905, the Menominee were cutting about twenty-five million **board feet** a year. A board foot equals a piece of lumber twelve inches long and twelve inches wide and one inch thick. That's a lot of wood!

At the request of the Menominee, U.S. Senator Robert M. La Follette of Wisconsin got a law passed that was supposed to help the tribe's forest. This law directed the U.S. Forest Service to recognize logging on the Menominee Reservation as **sustained-yield forestry** . This meant that the Menominee could continue their tradition of selectively cutting *only* mature trees.

sustained-yield forestry: An organized plan to replant and regrow trees that are cut down

Menominee lumberjacks

But, the commercial loggers and government foresters wanted to clear-cut the forest, which meant they would cut down *all* the trees. Forest Service officials built a single large, expensive sawmill that could produce much more timber than the Menominee people wanted to cut.

As a result, the Menominee had to pay for a sawmill that was too big for their needs. Despite the protests of the tribe, entire sections of the Menominee Forest were clear-cut. Eventually, the U.S. government awarded the Menominee Nation $8.5 million for their losses, but it wouldn't be for nearly twenty more years.

In 1934, the Menominee brought a **lawsuit** against the Forest Service for harming their resources. By now, more than ten percent of the reservation had been clear-cut. Federal foresters had not replanted the cutover areas as they had promised. They also failed to get rid of the brush. These failures led to forest fires that further damaged the forest.

In that same year, the Indian Reorganization Act ended the programs that were designed to make Indians live like non-Indians. Most Indian boarding schools closed. Indian governments, which had been shut down, were allowed to reorganize and create new **constitutions**. However, some U.S. congressmen still wanted to "free" American Indian

lawsuit: A case before a court of law that seeks money for damages done to someone ◆ **constitutions:** Formal written laws and plans of government

people from life on the reservation and bring them into the rest of American society. This idea was called **termination** (tur mih **na** shun). Terminating the reservation would also "free" the government from its responsibilities to protect American Indian people and their property. In other words, the government would not have to do what it had promised the American Indians in the treaty.

Twenty years later in 1953, the U.S. Congress passed a law that laid out the goals of termination. One goal was to relocate or move Indian people from rural reservations to urban areas. In cities, job training programs and help with housing were supposed to be available. But when Menominee people chose to move, most received only one-way bus tickets to Chicago, Milwaukee, or St. Paul!

The Menominee were told that if they did not support termination, Congress would terminate them anyway within three years. In 1954, Congress passed the Menominee Termination Act, which created Menominee County.

The tribe had four choices for their lands. First, the lands could become a national forest. Second, the land could become a state forest. Third, once tribal lands had been allotted to individuals, the property could become part of Shawano and Oconto counties. Or fourth, the Menominee Reservation could become a county of the state of Wisconsin. The Menominee chose the last option.

termination: The ending of something

In 1959, Governor Gaylord Nelson signed a settlement creating Menominee County. The Menominee Nation used most of its $8.5 million settlement to turn the reservation into a real county, creating county roads, schools, law enforcement, courts, and parks. When the tribe was officially terminated in 1961, the $8.5 million had been spent. Menominee County immediately became the poorest county in the state.

In 1952, Governor Nelson signed the bill creating Menominee county.

The Menominee changed the way they managed the forest by creating Menominee Enterprises Incorporated (MEI). It was set up like a business with a board of directors. Some of the directors were not Menominee. They controlled the board and made decisions that some Menominee did not like. The board offered to sell some of the tribe's land along the Wolf River to the state of Wisconsin for a public campground. Then the board decided to make a man-made lake and rent homes around it to tourists.

Ada Deer and DRUMS

Ada Deer grew up on the Menominee Reservation in the 1940s and 1950s. She loved learning and went on to the University of Wisconsin in Madison. In the late 1960s, when she was a college student, she became active in a group called **DRUMS**. DRUMS was organized by some Menominee members to protest the actions of the

MEI. DRUMS sent Ada Deer to Washington, D.C., to try to persuade Congress to end termination and to **restore** the tribe. She later became Assistant Secretary of the Interior and Director of the Bureau of Indian Affairs. Appointed in 1993, Ada Deer is the first American Indian to hold this high office. She went from Washington to go back to the University of Wisconsin in Madison, where she now teaches American Indian studies and social work.

James White, President of DRUMS, speaks a protest

Then in 1968, the board decided to sell the land around the lake. DRUMS protested by marching from Keshena to the state capitol in Madison. DRUMS also filed lawsuits in the U.S. court, claiming that the dams required for the project would flood streams and marshes and would hurt wildlife habitats. To prevent land sales, Menominee elders and others lay down along the highway that led to the real-estate office. In 1969, Congress passed the Menominee Restoration Bill, which officially restored the tribe.

restore: To bring something back to its original condition

Menominee Life Today

The Menominee have struggled to rebuild after the terrible effects of termination. Following the passage of the National Indian Gaming Act in 1988, the Menominee Nation opened a **casino**, bingo hall, and hotel complex in Keshena. With **gaming dollars**, they have built a new health clinic and schools. The tribe has taken control of several important programs that had been run by the state and U.S. governments. The Menominee Nation is now one of two Indian nations in Wisconsin to operate its own tribal community college. The College of the Menominee Nation educates both Native and non-Native students.

Today, the Menominee who live on the reservation are more sucessful economically. This is largely because of the money made by their gaming and forest industries. Now that they manage the forest themselves, the Menominee have gone back to the advice of their elders. They only cut mature timber selectively from east to west. People consider the Menominee forest one of the most beautiful and healthy forests on earth. Forest managers from all over the world visit it and are amazed by the many kinds of trees of different ages, including four-hundred-year-old hemlocks. Recently, a space shuttle astronaut described a large green patch west of Lake Michigan as a "jewel." His observation did not surprise the Menominee. It was their forest.

Photo by Patty Loew

College of the Menominee Nation

casino: Building where gambling and other entertainment takes place ◆ **gaming dollars:** Money made in the gambling industry, generally from casinos

Remembering

Today, the Menominee people continue to speak their language and practice their traditions and traditional religion. In recent years, the Menominee have even brought back the centuries-old sturgeon ceremony. The ceremony includes songs, an ancient fish dance to honor the return of the sturgeon, and a feast to thank the Creator. This tradition had been halted when dams, which were built on the Wolf River below the reservation, blocked the sturgeon from reaching the reservation. With sturgeon supplied by the Wisconsin Department of Natural Resources, the ceremony continues regularly. The Menominee people hope that someday the dams will be torn down so that fish can swim freely into reservation waters.

Photo courtesy of Alan Caldwell

Educator and Elder Alan Caldwell at a Menominee pow wow

49

Chapter 4

The Ho-Chunk Nation

◆ ◆ ◆

The land in Wisconsin is full of clues about those who have lived on it, especially the Ho-Chunk people. Their stories, songs, effigy mounds, rock art, and place names remind us of the thousands of years that Wisconsin has been home to Ho-Chunk people and their ancestors. Most of their traditional tribal lands were located south and west of present-day Green Bay. Ho-Chunk territory, in fact, extended all the way to northern Illinois.

By the middle of the 1800s, though, treaties with the United States government had stripped away nearly seven million acres of land from the Ho-Chunk Nation. Today, the tribe is the only Wisconsin Indian Nation that is **recognized by the U.S. government** that is without reservation lands in the state. Even though the U.S. government removed them from their homeland again and again, many Ho-Chunk people returned to live on the land of their ancestors.

Ho-Chunk elder Bertha Blackdeer creates traditional baskets.

Photo by Lewis Koch for the Wisconsin Folk Museum Woodland Indian Project, Courtesy of UW-Madison Folklore Program

recognized by the U.S. government: When the tribal government and the U.S. government have a government-to-government relationship

Think about It

Why did the U.S. government want the Ho-Chunk people to leave? Why did the Ho-Chunk people keep coming? Where do members of the Ho-Chunk Nation live now? How do they celebrate or keep their traditions alive today?

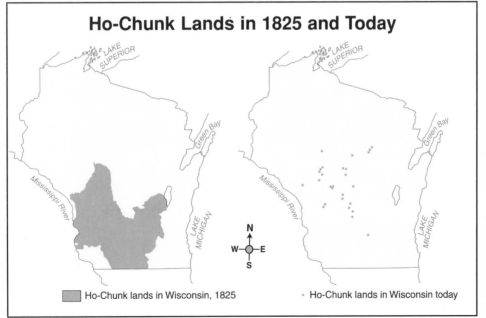

Ho-Chunk Lands in 1825 and Today

LAKE SUPERIOR

Green Bay

Mississippi River

LAKE MICHIGAN

N
W—E
S

LAKE SUPERIOR

Green Bay

Mississippi River

LAKE MICHIGAN

■ Ho-Chunk lands in Wisconsin, 1825

▪ Ho-Chunk lands in Wisconsin today

Map by Amelia Janes, Midwest Educational Graphics

Tribal Traditions

Hochungra (ho **chun** gruh) is the name used by members of the Ho-Chunk Nation to describe themselves. It means "people of the big voice" or "people of the sacred language." Unlike the other tribes in Wisconsin today, the Ho-Chunk speak a Siouan language.

Members of the Ho-Chunk Nation are organized by clans, each with special responsibilities. Twelve different clans exist today. They are divided into earth clans and sky clans. The earth division includes the Bear Clan. In the past, the Ho-Chunk picked a Bear Clan member to be their chief in times of war. The Bear Clan also made decisions about their land. The sky division includes the Thunderbird Clan. Peace chiefs came from this group.

Together, the leaders of the Bear and Thunderbird clans governed with the help of a council made up of members of each clan. The council guided everyday activities in the large villages. The Bear and Thunderbird Clan leaders were very important to their people. Many of the effigy mounds in

WHERE DOES THE NAME HO-CHUNK COME FROM?

The Ho-Chunk used to be known as the Winnebago, which is a word that comes from a Mesquakie word meaning "people of the stinking water." The Mesquakie chose this name because it described the smell of the waters near where the Ho-Chunk lived. They did not mean the name to be an insult. At certain times of the year, the waters of the Fox River and Lake Winnebago filled with smelly algae (al jee), and the awful stench made its way into the nearby Ho-Chunk villages.

algae: Small plants without roots or stems that live in water or on damp surfaces

Tshi-Zun-Hau-Kau,
Ho-Chunk Warrior

Ker-O-Menée,
Ho-Chunk Chief

Wa-Kaun,
Ho-Chunk Chief

Wisconsin were built in the forms of thunderbirds and bears. This could be a **coincidence** (co **in** sih dents), but maybe not. What do you think?

Bear Effigy mound near Lake Koshkonong

 Tribal History

Early Days

Generation after generation of Ho-Chunk men hunted animals for the meat and hides. The women gathered plants for food and medicines in Wisconsin's woods and meadows. Sometimes the Ho-Chunk hunted for buffalo west of the Mississippi River. The Ho-Chunk were farming their land at least a thousand years ago. They planted fields of corn, beans, and squashes.

coincidence: Something that happens by chance

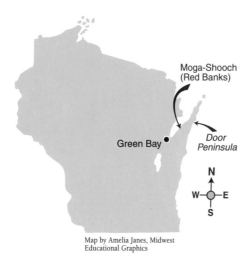

Moga-Shooch (Red Banks)

Green Bay

Door Peninsula

N
W—E
S

Map by Amelia Janes, Midwest Educational Graphics

The Ho-Chunk people felt a special bond with the animals and plants that provided them life.

The Ho-Chunk believe they originally came from **Moga Shooch** (mo gah **shooch,** Red Banks) on the Door peninsula not far from present-day Green Bay. The Ho-Chunk people formed the most powerful tribe in the area. Sometime in the century before the Europeans arrived, the Anishinaabe began moving into the northern part of Ho-Chunk territory. When the Anishinaabe arrived, the Ho-Chunk people moved farther south. This made the tribes living there angry. With no place to expand, the Ho-Chunk Nation split apart.

Sometime around the year 1570, a group of Ho-Chunk headed west down the Wisconsin River and across the Mississippi River to present-day Iowa. Once there, they separated into three different tribes: the Iowa, Oto, and Missouri. The Ho-Chunk people who remained in Wisconsin stayed together in large villages near Green Bay. From there, they could defend their homeland against the Anishinaabe from the north and the Illinois tribes from the south.

The Ho-Chunk at first welcomed the Europeans and the chance to trade furs for metal pots, knives, blankets, cloth, and guns. Unfortunately, this welcome eventually led to disaster. Many Ho-Chunk died from new diseases, such as smallpox, that had been brought by the Europeans. The Ho-Chunk people enjoyed using pots, blankets, guns, and other European trade goods, but using these items changed traditional tribal ways of living. Natural resources also began to disappear. After many years of hunting for the fur trade, Ho-Chunk hunters found fewer and fewer fur-bearing animals to trap.

In the late 1700s, trading lead, a mineral, became more important than trading furs. Ho-Chunk lands in southwestern Wisconsin contained rich deposits of **galena** (guh **lee** nah). As European-Americans heard about the richness of the galena deposits, the Ho-Chunk saw more and more non-Indian miners enter their territory. Old Grayheaded Decora, a Ho-Chunk leader, said that these miners moving in were "like wolves in the Plains to the dead buffalo." He also mentioned that the miners "spread out in every direction and began to dig and find and carry off lead on the Winnebago lands." By 1825, more than ten thousand miners had moved illegally into Ho-Chunk lands in southern Wisconsin.

Birchbark wigwams and canoes near Wisconsin Dells early in the 1900s

Parts of a traditional Ho-Chunk male's dance outfit

---

galena: A grayish lead ore used for making ammunition and paint

55

MINING GALENA

The Native people of the area had mined galena for at least eight thousand years. Women of the Ho-Chunk, as well as Sauk and Mesquakie Nations, mined galena every spring and fall. They gathered enough of the mineral for personal use and sometimes collected enough to trade with other Indians. The Ho-Chunk melted galena and used it as body paint, keeping the finest pieces to bury with their dead.

Galena

More and more non-Indians entered Ho-Chunk lands without permission. Tensions between the Ho-Chunk people and non-Indian settlers grew. In June 1827, the Ho-Chunk began to hear rumors that several of the tribe's warriors had been killed at Fort Snelling (now St. Paul) in the Minnesota Territory. Red Bird, a Ho-Chunk war chief, decided to take revenge.

Ho-Chunk women mined lead.

First Red Bird killed several non-Indians who had settled without permission on Ho-Chunk lands south of La Crosse. Later, in the same area, he attacked a barge carrying miners. For three months, the Ho-Chunk refused to turn over Red Bird to the white government. But eventually the Ho-Chunk convinced him to surrender. In September 1827, Red Bird gave himself up to the U.S. Army in Portage. He did not want to spend his life in prison, but he died in jail. Red Bird's courage made him a hero to many Ho-Chunk.

Red Bird's surrender

Giving Up Land

The government began putting pressure on the Ho-Chunk to cede some of their lead-rich lands. But the Ho-Chunk learned that U.S. officials wanted *all* their mineral lands south of the Wisconsin River. "Do you want *our* Country? Yours is much larger than ours," said Ho-Chunk speaker Little Elk to the government's representatives. "Do you want *our* wigwams? You live in palaces. My fathers, what can be your **motive** (**mo** tiv)?" This meant that Little Elk wanted to know the reasons for their greed.

Some leaders of the Sauk people had also ceded land to the U.S. government. But not all Sauk people agreed with the arrangement. In 1832, a Sauk leader called Black Hawk and hundreds of Sauk men, women, and children tried to reclaim their tribal lands in northern Illinois. Frightened non-Indians called in the army. When Black Hawk saw the number of troops, he knew that he could not fight them and win. But when he sent men to surrender, soldiers misunderstood and shot them. Black Hawk and his people escaped north through Wisconsin, hiding from troops as they tried to return to the west side of the Mississippi River. The troops killed most of Black Hawk's people as they tried to cross the Mississippi River. That battle came to be known as the Bad Axe **Massacre** (**mass** uh ker).

massacre: A cruel act of killing innocent people

Black Hawk

The Black Hawk War divided the Ho-Chunk. Some supported the Sauk war chief. Others supported the non-Indians. Still others remained **neutral** (**new** trul). In the end, the Black Hawk War led to a further loss of lands for the Ho-Chunk. The U.S. government forced them to give up their lands south of the Wisconsin and Fox Rivers to the Rock River, including their cornfields, hunting grounds, and the important villages of De Jope (Madison) and Neesh (Wisconsin Dells).

Black Hawk's Route

Map by Amelia Janes, Midwest Educational Graphics

In exchange for these lands, the government promised the Ho-Chunk people land in western Iowa. Five years later, twenty Ho-Chunk men ceded the tribe's remaining lands east of the Mississippi River and agreed to move to the lands set aside for them in Iowa. Tribal leaders protested that only two of the signers were from the Bear Clan—the only clan with tribal authority to sign such a treaty. Not all Ho-Chunk were willing to leave Wisconsin.

neutral: Staying out of a disagreement or not taking sides

Ho-Chunk Removals

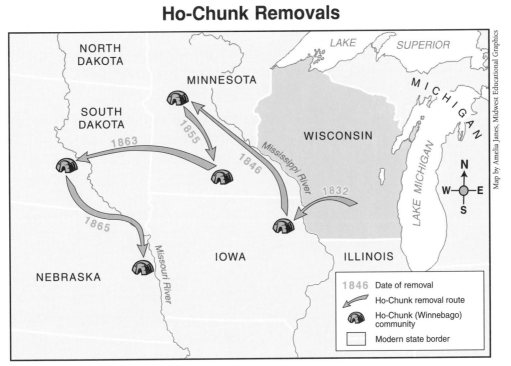

How many times were the Ho-Chunk people forced to move?

In 1837, the U.S. government offered land in northern Minnesota to the Ho-Chunk people. The government told them that the Minnesota land was better than the land in Iowa and that they had eight years to move there. Only after the tribe received a written copy of the agreement did they learn that the treaty actually read eight *months*. Some Ho-Chunk refused to leave their homelands. Others traveled to Iowa and Minnesota, but returned later to Wisconsin.

In 1855, the Ho-Chunk in northern Minnesota exchanged their lands for a reservation in the south-central part of Minnesota. The reservation was not very large, but the land was good for growing crops. Life was improving when the Civil War began in 1861. Many Ho-Chunk joined the Union Army. While they were off fighting, non-Indians near the reservation demanded that the Ho-Chunk be removed from Minnesota. As a result, the government forced the Ho-Chunk to move west to South Dakota where the land was very bare and very different from the land they were used to. When Ho-Chunk Chief Baptiste visited these lands, he told his people, "It is . . . cold country . . . no wood . . . bad country for Indians."

Even though the Ho-Chunk resisted, the government ordered them to move in the winter of 1863. The Ho-Chunk were not even allowed to wait for better weather. More than 550 of the nearly two thousand tribal members died on the way to South Dakota. Despite their hardship and sadness, the Ho-Chunk continued to resist removal. Most of the 1,382 survivors fled in dugout canoes down the Missouri River and took **refuge** (**ref** yooj) among the Omaha Indians in Nebraska. Two years later, this group of Ho-Chunk people signed a treaty that allowed them to purchase a portion of the Omaha reservation. They remain there to this day and are known as the Winnebago Tribe of Nebraska. Many Wisconsin Ho-Chunk people of today are the descendants of those who refused to move to reservations west of the Mississippi. Others are descendants of those who left and returned.

refuge: Protection or shelter from danger or trouble

The tough Ho-Chunk survivors who had hidden out and never left Wisconsin, or had returned from reservations in the west, were rounded up again and again in the late 1800s. But again and again, they returned home to Wisconsin. Some who returned were led by Chiefs Dandy and Yellow Thunder. Yellow Thunder had managed to buy a small piece of land where Ho-Chunk could live. In 1881, the United States Congress passed a special law that allowed the Wisconsin Ho-Chunk people forty-acre homesteads.

WHS Archives, ph6062a

Yellow Thunder outside his wigwam.

Yellow Thunder around 1880

WHS Archives

Dealing with Non-Indians

When Europeans first met the Ho-Chunk and other Native people, the Europeans did not understand the Native way of life. They did not understand the special relationship that Ho-Chunk people shared with the animals, the land, and the water. Many Europeans felt that Native Americans should become Christians and worship in their churches. In the 1600s French missionaries had established **missions** to try to convince the Ho-Chunk to become Catholic. Then, in the late 1800s, the Evangelical Reformed Church began a mission school near Black River Falls. After that, Norwegian

Photo by Bobbie Malone

Yellow Thunder's memorial marker in Baraboo

missions: Places of worship where missionaries live and work

Missionaries traveled with Native people to reach Wisconsin.

Lutherans started a mission and boarding school near Wittenberg in Shawano County. Some Ho-Chunk people did become Christians. Some blended Christian and Native traditional beliefs. Others held to their own Native beliefs.

The United States government also opened boarding schools to teach non-Indian ways of life to Ho-Chunk children. One of these was the Tomah Indian Industrial School. Here, teachers discouraged Ho-Chunk children from speaking their Native language and from expressing their Native culture, such as wearing traditional clothing. Often, children as young as six years old were taken from their homes, placed in the Tomah school, and not allowed to return home until after they had graduated from high school! Can you imagine saying goodbye to your family when you were only six years old and not returning home for so many years? How do you think you would feel? How would you feel when you finally returned home?

The Ho-Chunk people had a hard time making a living on poor land. Their homesteads were on land that was not good for farming. Most Ho-Chunk managed to feed their families by hunting, gathering, fishing, and gardening. Before the Ho-Chunk were removed, they had gathered cranberries on their ancestral homelands. Now these cranberry marshes were the private property of non-Indians. Sometimes Ho-Chunk members hired themselves out as farm helpers or worked in the cranberry fields.

By the early 1900s, many Ho-Chunk people had returned to the Wisconsin Dells area. Others had never left. Non-Indian people began vacationing there to enjoy the natural beauty of the Wisconsin River and its sandstone cliffs. As a result, some Ho-Chunk people found a way to make a living from

The Ho-Chunk people have always harvested cranberries.

these tourists. Some Ho-Chunk members entertained the tourists with traditional songs and dances at the Stand Rock Ceremonial. Shops and trading posts also sold souvenirs made by Ho-Chunk members, such as wood carvings and beautiful baskets made from the black ash tree. Photographs and postcards of Ho-Chunk tribal members were also sold. Wisconsin Dells is still one of Wisconsin's most popular tourist areas, and people who go there can still see the beauty of the Dells and appreciate the Ho-Chunk ties to the area.

The Ho-Chunk people have always had their own form of governing themselves. But in 1934, the U.S. government passed a law that allowed tribes on reservations to create their own constitutional governments, more like that of the U.S. government. But

At the H. H. Bennett studio in the Wisconsin Dells, you will see photographs and post cards of Ho-Chunk people made to sell to visiting tourists.

would the Ho-Chunk people qualify if they did not have a reservation? Someone working for President John F. Kennedy in the 1960s learned of a small Ho-Chunk homestead that the government was protecting for the Ho-Chunk people. The government decided that this homestead would be enough to form land that could count as a "reservation." The amount of land that the tribe owns continues to grow as the Ho-Chunk Nation is able to purchase more property.

Tribal trust lands are lands held by a tribe to be used for the good of the tribe. Although individual Indians live on the lands, they do not own them. Reservation lands are the blocks of tribal trust lands that were defined in treaties.

 ## Ho-Chunk Life Today

Despite continued pressure to change, many members of the Ho-Chunk Nation still hold on to their own way of life. Today, Ho-Chunk conduct traditional feasts to celebrate and honor many things including the Creator, ancient traditions, the spirits, the people, the animals, the seasons, and tribal elders. Feasts often include drumming, dancing and singing. They give thanks to the Creator for providing for their needs. Today the 5,800 members of the Ho-Chunk Nation own more than two thousand acres of land scattered across twelve Wisconsin counties. Despite the problems of providing services to people spread out so far, the Ho-Chunk Nation operates many tribal programs, including health clinics

Photo by Lewis Koch for the Wisconsin Folk Museum Woodland Indian Project, Courtesy of UW-Madison Folklore Program

L-R: Lance Long, Gordon Thunder, and Elliot Walker form a group of traditional Ho-Chunk drummers.

Bison like these are now on Ho-Chunk lands near Muscoda.

and Head Start centers. The Ho-Chunk Nation assists businesses in each of its communities. The nation has bought land to be used for housing near Black River Falls, Wittenberg, Wisconsin Rapids, Tomah, and the Dells. The Ho-Chunk have also brought back a small herd of **bison** to the tribal trust lands along the Wisconsin River near **Muscoda** (**mus** kuh day). Today, the bison herd continues to grow. Bison meat is leaner and considered healthier than beef. Successful Ho-Chunk casinos in the Wisconsin Dells, Nekoosa, Black River Falls, and Madison help pay for these many programs and services for tribal members, young and old.

Remembering

The Ho-Chunk people have survived in Wisconsin. They have resisted many attempts by the U.S. government to remove them. They have had to give up their lands, but they have clung to their traditions. They are now buying land to restore bison and prairie. They have adapted or changed some of their traditions, but they are now working hard to teach their language and culture to their children. They respect the hard work of their ancestors and tribal elders, and they want non-Indians to learn about and respect the Ho-Chunk way of life.

Ho-Chunk Elder Owen Cloud in pow wow outfit

bison: Buffalo

Chapter 5

The Ojibwe Nation

◆ ◆ ◆

The Anishinaabe remember a time when they lived "on the shore of the Great Salt Water in the East." But oral tradition explains that this land on the coast of the Atlantic Ocean had not always been their home. The original homes of the Anishinaabe—the Ojibwe, Odawa, and Potawatomi—were in the lands that border the Great Lakes.

Long ago the Creator, **Gitchi-Manitoo** (**gih** tchee man ih **to**), had placed the Anishinaabe on the shores of the Great Lakes and taught them everything they needed to know. But over time, the people forgot these lessons and began to quarrel among themselves, so Gitchie-Manitoo told them to leave. The Anishinaabe moved east and were gone so long they forgot the way home!

Sometime later, they understood that the time had come to return home. Gitchie-Manitoo told them to follow a Sacred Shell that would lead them to the place where the "Food Grows on Water."

As the Anishinaabe began to move west, they separated into three groups of people.

The Odawa went north and eventually settled in the upper peninsula of Michigan and in Canada, where some remain today. Others were removed to Oklahoma. The

Potawatomi stayed mostly south, settling in the Ohio Valley and around the southern borders of the Great Lakes. The Ojibwe moved into the northern portions of Michigan, Minnesota, and Wisconsin.

The Anishinaabe left their homes along the Atlantic coast thousands of years ago! As they moved west, some people stayed at places where they stopped along the way. Those Anishinaabe that kept traveling eventually came to the south shore of Lake Superior. There, according to their traditional stories, they found **manoomin** (muh **noh** min), or wild rice. This was the "Food that Grows on Water." The final stop for the Anishinaabe was an island they called **Mo-ning-wun-a-kawn-ing** (mo ning won a **kaw** ning), which means "the place of the gold-breasted woodpecker." The Anishinaabe later renamed it, Madeline Island, in honor of the eldest daughter of the chief of the Crane Clan. She had married a French fur trader and had taken the Christian name of Madeline. But this is not the place where the Ojibwe people would stay. In fact, the tribe did not even remain a single group.

Think about It

What made the place where "food grows on water" so important to the Ojibwe people? What happened to the people on Madeline Island? Why did they leave? Where did they go? Why did they not remain together? Where are the Ojibwe people today? This is the longest chapter in the book, but once you read it, you'll understand why!

Tribal Traditions

As with the Menominee and Ho-Chunk, the Ojibwe people organized themselves by clans. The seven original clans were the Crane, Loon, Fish, Bear, Marten, Deer, and Bird. The Crane and Loon Clans supplied the chiefs who shared leadership. The Fish Clan provided the thinkers and the problem-solvers. The Marten Clan produced warriors, and the Deer Clan provided poets. Members of the Bear Clan were protectors of the community. Some members of the Bear Clan guarded the village, while others learned about medicines and used their knowledge to heal people. The Bird Clan provided the spiritual leaders.

Ojibwe Migration to Wisconsin

Map by Amelia Janes, Midwest Educational Graphics

Photo by Rick March, Wisconsin Arts Board Collection

WHAT'S THE DIFFERENCE BETWEEN THE NAMES OJIBWE AND CHIPPEWA?

Europeans called the Ojibwe people, **"Chippewa"** (chih puh wah). This name appears in the Chippewa Treaty Rights and in place names, such as Chippewa Falls. There are differing versions of what the word Ojibwe means. Although some think it refers to the puckered-style seams on the traditional tribal moccassins, many elders say comes from the Algonquian word that means "to script." This refers to the picture writing the Ojibwe developed, which became the main written language of trade.

St. Croix Ojibwe member Margaret Hart beaded these moccasins.

Life among the Ojibwe bands, then as now, followed the seasons. In early spring, the people speared fish and made maple sugar or syrup. To make maple sugar or syrup, they quickly boiled the sap from the maple tree over a fire. Then, they reduced the heat, until the sugar turned to syrup. Maple syrup and sugar could be eaten alone, or mixed into other foods, or stored for later use. In the summer, Ojibwe men fished and hunted, while the women gathered plant foods and tended gardens of corn, beans, squash, and potatoes. During late summer, families began preparing to harvest wild rice. During wintertime, the

Do you think this fish decoy will do the job?

Lac du Flambeau Ojibwe John Snow finishes his carved decoy for ice-fishing.

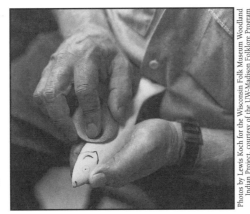

Photos by Lewis Koch for the Wisconsin Folk Museum Woodland Indian Project, courtesy of the UW-Madison Folklore Program

women made clothes for their entire families. Ojibwe men hunted white-tailed deer and trapped beaver, otter, and other fur-bearing animals. They would cut holes in the lake ice and fish for **muskie (muskellunge, mus** kuh lunj) and pike using wooden decoys, spears, or nets under the ice.

Wild rice is important to the Ojibwe people. It reminds them of the traditional story about their ancestors following the sacred shell to the place where "Food Grows on Water." Used alone or in soups, stews, and pancakes, wild rice is a very healthy and useful food.

In late summer, harvesting rice involves the whole family. First, everyone prepares the wild rice beds by tying bundles of rice stalks together. After the rice ripens completely, pairs of tribal members paddle their canoes to the rice beds. In the past, tribal members would shake the rice from the bundles of stalks. Today, tribal and state laws say ricing sticks must be used to remove the rice from the stalks. One person poles or slowly and carefully paddles through the

In the wild rice sloughs on the Bad River Reservation. As one boy poles the canoe, the other person carefully knocks the wild rice into the boat.

shallow water, while the other person uses two special ricing sticks to gently knock the rice kernels onto the floor of the canoe. The two people then spread the rice over woven mats and leave it for a day or two to dry before roasting, or **parching**, it. Traditionally, men or boys wearing clean moccasins would "dance" the rice— tramping on it with a shuffling motion in clay- or buckskin-lined pits—to loosen the chaff from the kernel. Today, rubber-soled shoes are sometimes used instead of moccasins, and the pits in which the rice is "danced" are lined with concrete instead of buckskin or clay. Finally, the rice is tossed in shallow birch bark baskets to separate the broken husks from the kernels. This tossing is called **winnowing** (**wih** no wing).

Tribal History

Early Days

The Ojibwe people welcomed the Frenchmen who arrived in the early 1600s. With European guns, the Ojibwe became better hunters.

The Ojibwe liked the French. The tribe welcomed them into their communities and even adopted many into their own families. Many Frenchmen married Ojibwe women. Their children became part of the Marten or Wolf Clans, the warriors. The Ojibwe fought alongside their French allies throughout the 1600s. The Ojibwe and French fought against the English and their allies, the Five Nations.

Madeline Island was a major trading post for the Ojibwe Nation. It was also its spiritual center. The three tribes of the Anishinaabe—the Ojibwe, the Potawatomi, and the Odawa—returned to the island at various times throughout the year to conduct **Midewiwin** or Grand Medicine Lodge ceremonies. The Midewiwin

---

parching: Making something very dry by roasting ◆ **winnowing:** To separate chaff by blowing with air

ceremonies had their own songs and stories. The Midewiwin contained the spiritual heritage of the Anishinaabe, and it provided the people with a code of conduct that explained the ways the people were supposed to behave. This code of conduct was a belief system that helped the Anishinaabe stay strong in body, mind, and heart.

Shing-Gaa-Ba-W'osin, an Ojibwe Chief

By the 1660s, Jesuit missionaries established a mission on Madeline Island. These "Black Coats" wanted the Ojibwe people to become Christians. Some became Christians, while others resisted. Soon, the differences in spiritual beliefs divided the people. Some bands of Ojibwe decided to leave the island. The ones who stayed became ancestors of the Bad River and Red Cliff Ojibwe Bands.

In search of furs to trade, groups of Ojibwe began moving farther inland. As the Ojibwe moved away from Lake Superior, they grew closer to the Mesquakie and Dakota peoples. This caused problems among the tribes. Every winter, some Ojibwe traveled south and west to the **St. Croix** (saynt **croy**) and Chippewa River valleys to hunt deer, moose, elk, and other animals. Every summer, they returned to Madeline Island for the Midewiwin ceremonies.

The Ojibwe sometimes fought with the Dakota. At other times, they lived together peacefully. But by the early 1800s, they were fighting constantly. In 1825 the United States invited the Ojibwe, Dakota, and other Indian nations to meet at Prairie du Chien to negotiate a treaty of "peace and friendship." As it turned out, the treaty was the first step toward getting the tribes to give up their lands.

Giving Up Land

Treaties were not easy to make with the Lake Superior Ojibwe. They did not have a single chief with whom U.S. government officials could negotiate. Each Ojibwe band had several leaders who governed by consent of the people. Forty-one Ojibwe tribal leaders signed the treaty at Prairie du Chien.

The Ojibwe and other tribes gathered at Prairie du Chien to sign the Treaty of 1825.

In the treaties of 1837 and 1842, the U.S. government pressured the Ojibwe to give up many acres of land. This meant nearly two-thirds of present-day northern Wisconsin, a portion of central Minnesota, and much of Michigan's Upper Peninsula! In exchange for the land, the government paid the Ojibwe small **annuities** (ah **new** uh teez) and trade goods. But these treaties were very unfair to the Ojibwe people. The U.S. gained billions of board feet of timber, billions of tons of iron ore, and fifteen thousand lakes. For giving up the land that provided their traditional way of life, the Ojibwe received only a little bit of money.

The Native ideas about the land exchange were very different from the U.S. government's idea. The Ojibwe believed they were merely *leasing* their land, not *selling* it. In an 1864 **petition** (puh **tih** shun) they brought to Washington, D.C., the

annuities: Yearly payments ◆ **petition:** A letter signed by a large number of people requesting that something or someone change

Illustration by Henry Rowe Schoolcraft

In this petition from Ojibwe clan chiefs, the lines link the animals' hearts and eyes to a chain of wild rice lakes in the original Ojibwe homeland. What does this petition tell you about how the Ojibwe people felt about giving up their land?

Ojibwe insisted they had sold *only* the right to cut timber: "From the usual height of cutting a tree down and upwards to top is what I sell you . . . I reserve the root of the tree." The Ojibwe people did not believe that they had sold the land itself.

The Ojibwe began to worry about protecting the land for their children, grandchildren, family, and friends who would follow. In both the 1837 and 1842 treaties, the Ojibwe reserved important rights: the right to hunt, fish, and gather on the land they ceded to the United States government. In exchange, the U.S. government promised the Ojibwe people that they would not be removed from their land as long as they did not "misbehave." This promise was not kept.

In February of 1850, President Zachary Taylor signed a removal order. In an effort to force the Ojibwe to move, officials of the U.S. government changed the place where the tribe would receive its 1850 annuity payments. Instead of Madeline Island, the usual place, the Ojibwe were forced to travel all the way to Sandy Lake, Minnesota.

In the fall and winter of that year, more than four hundred Ojibwe people traveled 1,100 miles to receive their payments. One hundred seventy people died from starvation, disease, and the cold at Sandy Lake. Two hundred thirty more people died on the way home to their villages. Chief Buffalo said, "Our women and children do indeed cry, our Father [the president], on account of their suffering from cold and hunger." In an 1851 letter sent to the government, Chief Buffalo stated, "We wish to . . . be permitted to remain here where we were promised we might

Ojibwe Journey to Sandy Lake

Map by Amelia Janes, Midwest Educational Graphics

live, as long as we were not in the way of the Whites."

For the next two years, Ojibwe chiefs and other leaders begged officials in Washington, D.C. to reconsider the removal order. In the spring of 1852, Chief Buffalo, who was then ninety-three years old, traveled by foot, canoe, and railroad to the U.S. capitol. When he arrived, Chief Buffalo met with President Millard Fillmore. President Fillmore smoked the peace pipe out of respect for Chief Buffalo and for those who came with him. Chief Buffalo and Chief O-sho-ga explained that the Ojibwe had been told that the U.S. government was not interested in Ojibwe *land,* just the pine trees and the minerals to be found there. The Ojibwe people believed that they had never ceded the land itself. President Fillmore believed what the chiefs said, and he stopped the removal order.

In 1854, Ojibwe chiefs and other tribal leaders gathered for the last time for treaty talks with U.S. negotiators. Ojibwe leaders insisted that they have a number of reservations around the state. They also insisted that the Ojibwe Nation keep the rights to hunt, fish, and gather on the land they had agreed to give up. In these negotiations, the Ojibwe created four reservations in Wisconsin: Bad River, **Lac Courte Oreilles** (lah **coo** duh ray), **Lac du Flambeau** (**lack** du **flam** bo), Red Cliff and Bad River. But of the millions of acres of original Ojibwe homeland, less than 275,000 acres remained after the 1854 treaty.

Chief Buffalo, Principal Chief of the Ojibwe, 1852

Leaders of the St. Croix and **Sokaogon** (suh **kog** uhn) or Mole Lake Ojibwe did not attend the treaty talks or, if they did, they did not sign the treaty. As a result, both the St. Croix and Mole Lake Ojibwe were *without land* for nearly eighty years before they finally got their own reservations.

By limiting the Ojibwe to just four reservations, the federal government tried to force the Ojibwe bands together, even though not all Ojibwe bands were alike. For example, the separate bands that had lived at Yellow River, Mud Lake, and Old Post became known simply as the Lac Courte Oreilles Band. Although the bands were Ojibwe, they had traditions of their own. When the groups became joined together, some of these traditions were either changed or lost.

Dealing with Non-Indians

The bands did share similar and painful experiences when the U.S. government tried to force them to give up their Indian ways. When the General Allotment Act was passed, the federal government divided up reservation land. Each tribal member received eighty acres. Ojibwe members

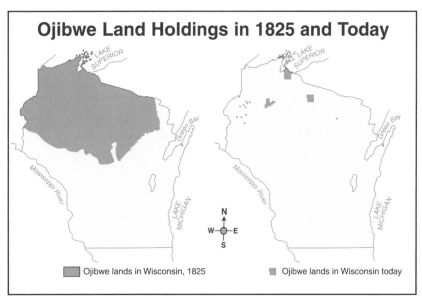

Ojibwe Land Holdings in 1825 and Today

☐ Ojibwe lands in Wisconsin, 1825   ☐ Ojibwe lands in Wisconsin today

Map by Amelia Janes, Midwest Educational Graphics

agreed not to sell their lands for twenty-five years. But land **speculators** (**speck** yoo la turs), who were being helped by government officials, found ways around the law. As a result, by the time the allotment program ended in 1934, the Ojibwe tribe had lost nearly half of their original reservation lands.

U.S. government officials took Ojibwe children from their homes and placed them in government boarding schools. School officials discouraged the children from speaking their language or practicing their religions and customs. Throughout much of the late 1800s and early 1900s, Ojibwe parents had no say in decisions about the schools their children attended. Most Ojibwe children went to one of three

speculators: People who try to make money by buying and selling

Indian Boarding School Locations in Wisconsin

Map by Amelia Janes, Midwest Educational Graphics

Girls at Lac du Flambeau Boarding School in 1890. How do you think students felt in these clothes?

government-run schools in Hayward, Tomah, or Lac du Flambeau. Some went to Christian mission schools, such as St. Mary's School on the Bad River Reservation. Other children were sent as far away as Pennsylvania.

These schools did not provide a good education for their Indian students. Some schools even included a work program that paid students poorly and kept them from returning home to their families during the summer. In spite of having their families pulled apart, the separate Ojibwe bands survived. Ojibwe communities in Wisconsin were able to preserve their tribal traditions and keep their tribal identities.

The Six Ojibwe Bands

The Lac Court Oreilles Band

In about 1745, three brothers of the Bear Clan led their families to an abandoned Odawa camp on the shore of Lac Courte Oreilles near present-day Hayward. These Ojibwe were followed by other Ojibwe families and settled on the Chippewa River. They named their settlement **Pahquahwong** (pa kwa **wong**), meaning "where the river is wide."

Before the 1854 treaty, Chief **Aw-ke-wain-ze** (ah key **wayn** zee) which means, "The Old Man," walked all the way around the reservation lands he had chosen for his people. He took great care to choose the area that contained the best wild rice beds.

Lac Court Oreilles Band

Map by Amelia Janes, Midwest Educational Graphics

WHERE DID THE NAME LAC COURTE OREILLES COME FROM?

The French always called Pahquahwong "Lac Courte Oreilles," which meant "Lake of the Short Ears." This name referred to the earlier Odawa people, who, unlike the Ojibwe, did not wear heavy earrings that stretched their ear lobes.

Unfortunately, things did not go smoothly for his people, even with this excellent land. Logging and dam projects by non-Indians destroyed the wild rice beds and even Pahquahwong itself.

In 1912, a power company began buying property near the reservation. This company planned to build a huge dam to provide power to the area. But, the dam would flood thousands of acres of reservation land. The dam would put maple groves, cranberry bogs, wild rice beds, cemeteries—even the village of Pahquahwong—underwater! The company promised to build a new village and to move Indian graves to higher ground. The company also promised to replant the wild rice beds and repay the Ojibwe back for the loss of their annual harvest.

The Lac Court Oreilles strongly objected to the power company's plans and tried to stop the project. Despite Indian protests, the federal government gave a license to the company to build and operate the dam. When the dam was completed, reservation lands began to fill with water. Soon the village was under twenty-five feet of water.

The company had broken its promises. Even worse, the Lac Courte Oreilles community learned that seven hundred Indian graves had been left behind and were now underwater. With the water level in the newly created lake now higher than ever, it was impossible to grow new rice beds. The "Food that Grows on Water" could not grow on this water.

The Lac du Flambeau Band

Sometime before 1745, Sha-da-wish, a chief of the Crane Clan, led his family to the headwaters of the Wisconsin River. Some years later, his son, Keesh-ke-mun (meaning Sharpened Stone), led the band south along the river to land near present-day Minocqua. The groups established their village where the Bear River flows out from Flambeau Lake. This village had wonderful natural resources. The Ojibwe found fresh water, fish, forest, plants, and animals to sustain them.

Lac du Flambeau was an important fur trade center for many years, first for the French, then for the British, and finally for the non-Indian Americans. By the late 1880s, railroad and stagecoach lines reached the area. Soon loggers, settlers, and businessmen

Lac du Flambeau Band

Map by Amelia Janes, Midwest Educational Graphics

WHERE DID THE NAME LAC DU FLAMBEAU COME FROM?

Oral tradition tells of a nearly blind old man who taught the Ojibwe how to "fire hunt" for fish. The Ojibwe speared fish at night by the light of birch bark torches. They called the fire hunters **Waswaagan** (wahs **wah** gun), and the community became known among the other bands as *Waswaaganing.* French fur traders who watched the spearing ritual called the village *Lac du Flambeau,* a name that means "Lake of the Torches."

Son of an Ojibwe guide with a young tourist

pushed into the region. Unfortunately, some of these newcomers were dishonest, and they cheated tribal members.

For the first part of the 1900s, life on the Lac du Flambeau Reservation was difficult for tribal members. Most of the forest had already been cut down for lumber, and fewer tribal members could get jobs as loggers. But the railroads that carried the logs away from the area now began to bring in tourists for summer vacations. Some Ojibwe men worked as hunting and fishing guides. Lac du Flambeau women earned money by selling beadwork, weavings, and baskets to the tourists. But the summer season was short, and most tribal members found it hard to make a living. Some could not afford the taxes on their land, and the government took their land from them. Others sold their land for much less than it was worth.

Some tribal members lost land in business deals with dishonest people. Non-Indian vacationers and **resort** (ree **zort**) owners now owned most of the tribe's best waterfront property. More and more, the Lac du Flambeau people found themselves outsiders on their own reservation.

The Red Cliff Band

The Ojibwe who remained on and around Madeline Island became known as the La Pointe Band, which was named for the island's main village. During the 1800s several leaders, including Chief Buffalo, became Christians. Under the leadership of Chief Buffalo, this band made its permanent home near the red cliffs of Buffalo Bay. This location was near the tribe's traditional fishing grounds.

resort: A place people go for vacations to rest and relax

Fishing remained very important to the Red Cliff Ojibwe. Tribal women made large nets from natural materials. Men carved cedar floats and stone sinkers. Ojibwe fishermen, in birch bark canoes, set their nets on deepwater reefs far offshore. As early as 1830, tribal fishermen were providing the American Fur

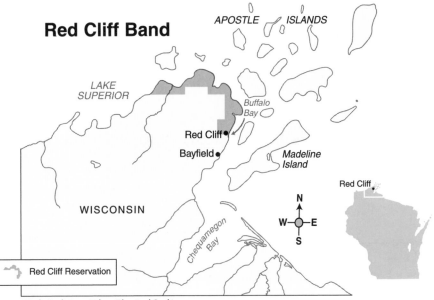

Red Cliff Band

APOSTLE ISLANDS

LAKE SUPERIOR

Buffalo Bay

Red Cliff

Bayfield

Madeline Island

WISCONSIN

Chequamegon Bay

Red Cliff

N
W — E
S

Red Cliff Reservation

Map by Amelia Janes, Midwest Educational Graphics

Company with lake trout and whitefish for food. But with their small boats and handmade nets, the Red Cliff Ojibwe could not compete with the large **commercial fleets** (kuh **mer** shuhl fleets) that came to Lake Superior's rich fishing waters. By the 1880s, the tribe's small fishing operation had fallen on hard times. More and more tribal members had to work for non-Indian fishing interests in nearby Bayfield.

Photo by Rick March, Wisconsin Arts Board Collection

Red Cliff Ojibwe member Marvin Defoe builds a birchbark canoe.

commercial fleets: Professional businesses that use fishing boats

Tribal logging began on the Red Cliff Reservation in the 1870s. Many Red Cliff tribal members found jobs as loggers and lumber mill workers. But within ten years, nearly all the timber was gone! Careless logging practices had left thousands of acres littered with brush piles. Sometimes lightning struck the brush piles, which would, in turn, start fires that would then burn thousands more acres. When the tribe's sawmill burned down in 1906, it was never rebuilt.

Some tribal members went to work for mining companies and shipping companies. A few returned to fishing. Others earned money by working in non-Indian shops and factories or by hiring themselves out as farmhands. By 1930, almost all (95%) tribal members had sold or lost their lands to non-Indians.

The Bad River Band

Unlike Chief Buffalo, some La Pointe chiefs did not become Christians. These La Pointe chiefs and their followers did not move to Red Cliff. Instead, they chose reservation lands southeast of La Pointe. This area along Lake Superior's south shore had good wetlands, which were rich with wild rice. The chiefs called their settlement simply **Odanah**—the Ojibwe word for "village."

The attempt to separate themselves from Christian teachings was not successful. Federal officials paid Protestant missionaries at Odanah to educate Indian boys and girls. Some years later, a group of nuns arrived and established a Catholic school, called St. Mary's. Because tribal

Bad River Band

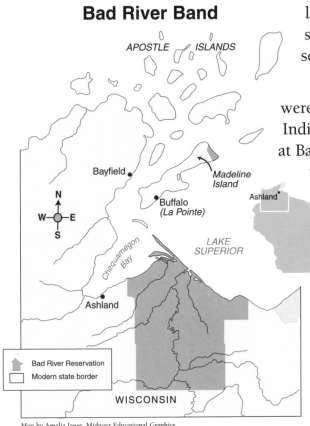

Map by Amelia Janes, Midwest Educational Graphics

leaders supported this school, most students went there, and the Protestant school eventually closed.

Many non-Indians in Northern Wisconsin were fair to the Ojibwe, but dishonest non-Indians made life difficult for tribal members at Bad River. A private company controlled all the timber business. The company and the U.S. government Indian agent cheated tribal members. By the end of the allotment period, the Bad River Band had lost nearly half of its original homelands.

The Sokaogan (Mole Lake) Band

The Ojibwe bands that traveled to Lac Courte Oreilles and Bad River set up their villages in areas full of wild rice. In the 1700s, another group of Ojibwe did the same, settling in an area near present-day Rhinelander that had full and promising wild rice beds. This area also had a lot of game and waterfowl. Nearby forests were filled with maple trees for sugar and birch trees from which they made canoes and containers.

Mole Lake Band

APOSTLE ISLANDS
Madeline Island
Crandon .

MICHIGAN

Wisconsin River

Brule River

Pine River

WISCONSIN

Rhinelander

Peshtigo River

Crandon

N
W—E
S

Wolf River

☐ Modern state border
🦫 Mole Lake Reservation

Map by Amelia Janes, Midwest Educational Graphics

Under the leadership of **Ki-chi-waw-be-sha-shi** (kitch chee **wah** bah shosh or The Great Marten), the Mole Lake Band grew to about seven hundred members. Ki-chi-waw-be-sha-shi became a powerful war chief. Because his band was recognized as the eastern guard of the Ojibwe, Mole Lake men protected the eastern borders of the Ojibwe Nation from enemy attacks. In 1806, the Dakota and Ojibwe fought their last major battle over control of the wild rice beds. More than five hundred Ojibwe and Dakota Indians died. They were buried together in a mass grave, which is still cared for by Mole Lake Elders today.

For reasons that are still unclear, **Migiizi** (meh **gee** zee), the Mole Lake leader, did not attend the treaty council in 1854. But the next year, he met with U.S. government officials and got them to promise to set aside twelve square miles for the Mole Lake homeland. However, the two copies of the map showing the reservation boundaries—one for the chief and one for the government files—got lost! Lacking proof of their agreement, the members of the Mole Lake Band were left homeless. In the

Ki-Chi-Waw-Be-Sha-Shi, Mole Lake Ojibwe leader

1920s, government reports described the Mole Lake Band as "starving and **destitute** (**des** tih toot)" Indians roaming Langlade and Forest counties.

The St. Croix Band

The St. Croix Band is the other "Lost Band" of Ojibwe people. After the Ojibwe left Madeline Island in the 1700s, some families traveled southwest. These families established dozens of villages along the St. Croix and Mississippi rivers. During the 1837 and 1842 treaties, the St. Croix had a distinct identity. The first treaty identifies chiefs **Bizhiki** (**bee** zhee key, The Buffalo) and **Ka-be-ma-be** (kah bay **mah** bay,

St. Croix Band Band

Map by Amelia Janes,
Midwest Educational Graphics

The Wet Month), and three warriors "from St. Croix river." However, none of the St. Croix chiefs signed the 1854 treaty. In fact, no record proves that they were ever at the meeting. In the eyes of the U.S. government, the St. Croix Band no longer existed. No one knows why the St. Croix were left out of the 1854 treaty and not given a reservation. Tribal historians suggest that perhaps Chief Bizhiki decided not to sign because the U.S. government had not lived up to its past promises. Whatever the reason, the St. Croix Band, like the Mole Lake Band, became landless and remained that way until the 1930s.

destitute: Lacking enough food, clothing, money, and shelter

Indian Reorganization and the Ojibwe Bands

In 1934, Congress passed the Indian Reorganization Act. Reorganization ended the allotment program and the Indian boarding school system. Now, all Ojibwe bands had the opportunity to reorganize their tribal governments. However, the newly created governments were not like traditional tribal structures. The government encouraged tribes to adopt constitutions that would make them similar to the way businesses are set up.

SOLDIERS AND PATRIOTIC AMERICANS

Even though American Indians were not allowed to become U.S. citizens until 1924, many Ojibwe men volunteered for military service in World War I. Ojibwe men also volunteered for military service in World War II. Their hunting and tracking skills were very useful, as was their complex language! The Thirty-Second ("Red Arrow") **Infantry** Division, in which many served in the South Pacific, made use of Ojibwe

WHS Archives, WHi(X3)18963

Indian veterans return to the Lac Courte Oreilles Reservation after WWI.

"code talkers." The Ojibwe language was unknown to the Japanese. Ojibwe women also contributed to the war effort by knitting and sewing for the Red Cross, buying war bonds, and growing extra food.

infantry: Foot soldiers

Still, reorganization offered the Ojibwe the chance to rebuild their communities and plan for the future. Reorganization also led to tribes being able to get back some of their land. In 1936, the St. Croix Ojibwe adopted a constitution and asked for land in Burnett and Polk counties. A year later, the Mole Lake Ojibwe did the same thing and received more than a thousand wooded acres on the eastern shore of Rice Lake in Forest County.

Children at the drum during the Winter Dam Protest at Lac Courte Oreilles, 1971

In the 1950s, the U.S. government policy known as "termination and relocation" was designed to remove American Indians from their reservations and into jobs in cities. Some Ojibwe people did leave their reservations and move to major cities. The change was difficult. The government did not keep promises to train people for jobs or to help them find good enough housing.

In the 1960s, some urban or city-dwelling Indians became active in the "Red Power" movement. Two Ojibwe brothers, Vernon and Clyde Bellecourt, co-founded the American Indian Movement (AIM) in Minneapolis. In 1971, Lac Courte Oreilles tribal members, with the help of AIM, protested at a dam near Hayward that had flooded their rice beds fifty years earlier! As a result, the Lac Courte Oreilles finally received money for some of the damages done by the dam. They also won the right to operate the dam.

The Battle over Spear-fishing

In the spring of 1974, the actions of two other Ojibwe brothers made major changes to Ojibwe history. Fred and Mike Tribble of the Lac Courte Oreilles Nation were arrested and charged with breaking Wisconsin conservation laws. The two had been caught with ice fishing equipment on a lake, which was off of their reservation but within territory to which the Ojibwe claimed hunting and fishing rights. "When they said I was doing it illegally," Mike Tribble recalled, "I took the treaty out of my back pocket and I said, 'No, I'm doing this under treaty rights.'"

The arrests prompted a lawsuit against the state of Wisconsin by the Lac Courte Oreilles Band. The band accused state officials of preventing the Ojibwe from **exercising** their rights to hunt, fish, and gather food in the ceded territory promised in their treaties. Five other Ojibwe bands joined the lawsuit.

Eventually, the six Ojibwe bands won their lawsuit. Through the 1990s, various U.S. court rulings redefined the Ojibwe treaty rights. A U.S. judge ruled that the Ojibwe—*not* the state—had the right to regulate tribal hunting and fishing off the

---

BOAT-LANDING PROTESTS

In 1975, members of different Ojibwe bands began spearing fish in lakes that were not on reservation land. This made many non-Indians angry, and they protested at boat landings. Thousands of people who protested the treaties tried to prevent tribal members from spearing walleye. Sometimes these protests turned violent. Tribal spear-fishers faced non-Indians who threw rocks, overturned their boats, and even fired guns at them. When their friends and relatives came to the landings to support the spear-fishers, they faced name-calling and rocks being thrown at them.

---

exercising: Putting into practice, as in exercising the right to vote

reservation. So, the Ojibwe created the Great Lakes Indian Fish and Wildlife **Commission** (cuh **mih** shun), known as GLIFWC (pronounced "glifwik"). GLIFWC manages the fish and wild rice harvests and provides information to the bands. The long legal battle finally ended in 1999. The U.S. Supreme Court agreed that the Lake Superior Ojibwe had the right to hunt, fish, and gather on ceded lands in Minnesota, Michigan, and Wisconsin.

Lake Superior Ojibwe Bands Today

Apart from the treaty rights struggle, perhaps the most important change that has happened in Ojibwe country has been the expansion of gaming. Beginning in the early 1990s, the Ojibwe opened casinos on all six of their reservations. The St. Croix Band's casinos, near Minnesota's Twin Cities, have made a lot of money for the tribe. Other casinos, in locations farther from major cities, such as the casino in Red Cliff, have not done very well.

Tinker Schuman teaches students how to make traditional leather pouches at the Lac du Flambeau Ojibwe School in 1997.

The Ojibwe people have used the money from their casinos to improve the quality of life on their reservations. On the Red Cliff and Mole Lake Reservations, for example, gaming has created jobs and funded tribal programs. On the Bad River Reservation, gaming dollars have helped pay for new tribal offices, water treatment facilities, and a hotel lodge. On the Lac du Flambeau and Lac Courte

---

commission: A group of people who meet together to solve a particular problem

91

Oreilles Reservations, casino money has helped improve education. The Lac du Flambeau Band built a new elementary school, and the Lac Courte Oreilles enlarged their elementary and high schools and funded the Lac Courte Oreilles Community College. In the Danbury and Hertel areas, the St. Croix Band has used gaming money to buy back some of their ancestral land.

Recent positive changes have given the Ojibwe a new sense of well-being about their future. Housing and social programs have improved living conditions on the reservations. Some communities are beginning to build an economic foundation designed to last, even if their casinos close. All the Ojibwe bands have put some of their gaming profits into environmental programs, which are run by the bands or through the Great Lakes Indian Fish and Wildlife Commission. Each band, for example, runs its own tribal fish hatchery and restocks not only lakes within its borders but also in lakes that are on lands they gave up in past years.

Lac du Flambeau Ojibwe John Snow with fish decoy

Remembering

Given the importance of wild rice, it is not surprising that every year the Ojibwe reseed more than six tons of wild rice into dozens of existing wild rice beds. They are also reestablishing historical rice stands. Preservation of the place where "Food Grows on Water" means a great deal to the Ojibwe people. Many Ojibwe people speak of the "seventh generation." This idea encourages tribal decision-makers to think about how their actions might affect those who followed—up to seven generations into the future. They remember how their ancestors protected them by preserving their rights to hunt and fish. Many Ojibwe leaders speak about the need to protect the environment for the next seven generations to come.

Chapter 6

The Potawatomi Nation

◆ ◆ ◆

Potawatomi oral tradition tells of three brothers: Ojibwe, the oldest, who was the Faith Keeper; Odawa, the middle brother, who handled trade; and **Bodewadmi** (bo deh **wahd** mee), the youngest, who kept the Sacred Fires lit. The three brothers became the **Neshnabek** (neh **shnah** bek or Anishinaabe)—the ancient alliance of Ojibwe, Odawa, and Potawatomi Nations. The Potawatomi still call themselves the "Keepers of the Fire."

In chapter 5, you learned that the Anishinaabe left their homes near the Atlantic coast to move back to the Great Lakes. During the long migration, the three "brother" tribes divided duties and responsibilities along traditional lines. As faith keepers, the Ojibwe carried the sacred Midewiwin scrolls. In charge of trade, the Odawa organized hunts and trade. As "Keepers of the Fire," the Potawatomi carried the sacred fire. Each job was important to the group's survival.

Oral tradition tells us that before the long journey back to the Great Lakes began, the three tribal "brothers" were one people. However, within a century of their return to the Great Lakes, the Ojibwe, Odawa, and Potawatomi people who had formed the Anishinaabe became three separate nations. Yet their languages are almost the same. Once back in the Great Lakes area, the Potawatomi lived on their homelands that covered parts of what is now known as lower Michigan, Ohio, Indiana, and Illinois.

Over time, all their land was taken. The Potawatomi people scattered, but they remained the "Keepers of the Fire."

Think about It

What was life like for the Potawatomi people when they reached the Great Lakes? How did the arrival of Europeans change the

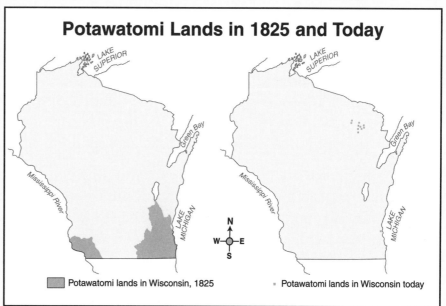

Potawatomi Lands in 1825 and Today

LAKE SUPERIOR

Green Bay

Mississippi River

LAKE MICHIGAN

N
W—◯—E
S

Potawatomi lands in Wisconsin, 1825

LAKE SUPERIOR

Green Bay

Mississippi River

LAKE MICHIGAN

Potawatomi lands in Wisconsin today

Map by Amelia Janes, Midwest Educational Graphics

Potawatomi way of life? What happened to the tribes' homelands? Where do the Potawatomi people make their homes in Wisconsin today?

Tribal Traditions

Like the other tribes in earlier chapters, the Potawatomi were organized into clans. Potawatomi people married someone outside of their clan. When couples married, they went to live with the husband's family in the village of his clan. However, Potawatomi children were also linked closely to the families of their grandfathers on their mothers' side. These close family ties on both sides made the bonds between villages stronger. Potawatomi people also often married other Anishinaabe—the Ojibwe and Odawa people. Such marriages between the tribes kept the Three Fires alliance stronger. During times of trouble, Potawatomi families and villages could depend upon many family members.

Photo by Lewis Koch for the Wisconsin Folk Museum Woodland Indian Project, Courtesy of the UW-Madison Folklore Program

Ned Daniels' granddaughter sleeps in her beaded cradleboard.

The seasons were, and still are, important to the Potawatomi people. In the summer, people lived in large villages at the edge of the forest near streams, lakes, or rivers where there would always be water and fresh fish. Women and children planted gardens and gathered berries and wild plants. In the fall, men hunted for deer, bears, raccoons, ducks, turkey, and geese. They also set traps for fur-bearing animals, especially minks and otters. During the fall, women and children also gathered nuts and fruits, such as cranberries, wild apples, and plums.

In the colder months, people built their wigwams in smaller camps, so that only a few people would depend on a limited food supply in any one place. Men continued to hunt, but winter was a time for many to stay indoors to prepare for the seasons ahead. Winter meant time to repair traps, work on crafts, and tell stories. Many of the traditional stories, especially stories that are spiritual, were not supposed to be told unless snow was on the ground.

When March came, it was time to collect and boil maple sugar. It was also time for spear fishing. Spring months got even busier. People came together in larger groups to hunt buffalo on the prairies or to fish in the streams. In May, the sturgeon began to "run." Although the Potawatomi count years by the winters, their year actually starts with the first run of fish up the river.

Spear fishing today

SUPERIOR CANOES

Because most of their travels took place on water, the Potawatomi like the Ojibwe, used lightweight canoes made of birchbark. The Potawatomi people used canoes for many purposes, the way we use pick-up trucks today. Birchbark canoes could store food and other cargo, and they were faster than the dug-out canoes used by many other tribes. Also, Potawatomi canoes were lighter, easier to carry, and easier to repair.

Tribal History

Early Days

Sometime before 1500, the Potawatomi migrated to the eastern shores of Lake Michigan. Over the next hundred years, they established more than a dozen villages in what is now the state of Michigan. Although much of their food came from hunting, fishing, and gathering, they began to rely more on farming—with gardens of corn, beans, and squash.

By the early 1600s, the Potawatomi had settled on the western shore of Lake Michigan in what is now Wisconsin. They were living on Washington and Rock Islands off the tip of the Door County Peninsula when they heard rumors about pale-skinned newcomers with "Hairy Faces" coming from the east. In 1634, the Potawatomi met Nicolet near present-day Green Bay. There tribal members were eager to trade furs for items such as metal knives, iron kettles, cloth, beads, and especially guns.

Washington Island, Rock Island, and Red Banks

Map by Amelia Janes,
Midwest Educational Graphics

Do you remember reading about the Huron people in chapter 2? Do you remember that they once handled the fur trade for the French? When the Five Nations defeated the Huron in the late 1640s, the Potawatomi began handling trade between the French and Great Lakes tribes. Then, the Potawatomi became the enemies of the Five Nations. To get furs from the Lake Michigan area to the French in Montreal, the Potawatomi filled their canoes with furs. Then they tied their canoes together to form a floating fleet and fought their way up the St. Lawrence River past Five Nations warriors. The Five Nations tried to stop this trade at its source, which was back in

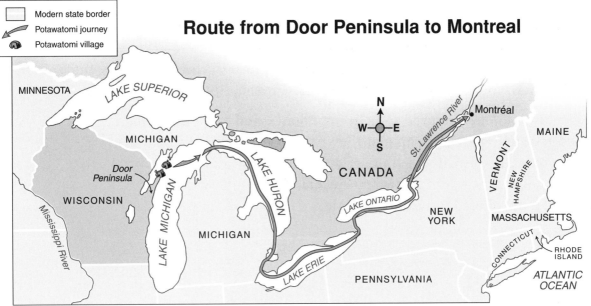

Route from Door Peninsula to Montreal

Map by Amelia Janes, Midwest Educational Graphics

Wisconsin. Using Dutch and English guns, Five Nations warriors made several attacks against the Potawatomi and their allies at their village on the Door Peninsula. Armed mostly with bows and arrows, the Potawatomi and their allies successfully defended themselves and their families.

Eventually the Five Nations signed a peace treaty with the French. In 1701, many of the tribes that had moved to safety in the Great Lakes area now returned to their homes in the east. By this time, the Potawatomi had settled more than fifty villages between northwestern Ohio and northern Illinois. They controlled an area of nearly three hundred million acres! But, as you will read in this chapter, many Potawatomi people would soon have no land at all!

The Potawatomi peacefully traded with the French for many years. Many French traders married Potawatomi women, which made ties between the two groups even stronger. When the French fought against the British in the French and Indian War (1754-1763), the Potawatomi supported the French. But the British won the war.

The British often refused to help the Potawatomi and other American Indian tribes get the trapping equipment they needed to hunt and to have furs to trade. Even worse, the British raised prices and limited the supply of several essential trading goods, such as gunpowder. But the Potawatomi were not the only Indian Nations that suffered under British rule.

In 1763, the Odawa war chief Pontiac organized an Indian movement to drive out the British. The Potawatomi joined and led successful attacks against British forts in the Great Lakes area. Although the movement ultimately failed, the British learned a valuable lesson. They started trading more like the French and even hired Frenchmen to conduct trade at certain British forts. Once again, the Potawatomi were able to get trade goods.

During the American Revolution (1775-1783), some Indian tribes remained neutral. Some joined the war on the American side. Most Potawatomi, however, fought with the British. They hoped the British would stop American settlers from moving farther west. But once again, the Potawatomi fought on the losing side. When the Americans defeated the British, the new U.S. government viewed the tribes as conquered enemies and made no attempt to control the non-Indian settlers. To defend their lands, the Potawatomi joined another Indian alliance of more than a dozen tribes and two thousand warriors. This alliance destroyed U.S. army troops along the Maumee River in Ohio.

Giving Up Land

In 1794, however, the Potawatomi were on the losing side for a third time. The Battle of Fallen Timbers in northwest Ohio crushed the power of the tribes and opened the Great Lakes area to non-Indian settlement. Between 1803 and 1807, the leaders of various Potawatomi bands signed treaties that ceded portions of Ohio, Indiana, Illinois, and the southeast portion of Lower Michigan.

In the early 1800s, an Indian religious leader known as "The Prophet" preached a return to traditional tribal values. The Prophet told his followers to give up non-Indian customs, religions, alcohol, and trade items. His brother, **Tecumseh** (teh **cum** suh), a Shawnee war chief, added his own message: Indian land was owned in common. No tribe had the right to sell land that belonged to all Indian people!

Support for Tecumseh and the Prophet grew strong among the Potawatomi. Main Poc, a Potawatomi war chief, invited the Prophet to move his village into Potawatomi

Tecumseh

country. He did so, and his settlement became known as Prophetstown. Tecumseh began using Prophetstown as his base while he visited other tribes. Tecumseh tried to organize the warriors of many tribes to challenge the U.S. army. In August 1811, before the alliance was strong enough, however, seven hundred warriors—most of them Potawatomi—attacked U.S. army troops near Prophetstown. The army burned Prophetstown and destroyed Potawatomi crops.

After the defeat at Prophetstown, many more Potawatomi joined Tecumseh. They offered help to the British in the War of 1812. Once again, they fought to keep American settlers away from the Great Lakes lands. But in supporting the British, the Potowatomi were defeated.

After the War of 1812, the Potawatomi way of life changed forever. Throughout the next eight years, the U.S. government forced the Potawatomi to give up land. Individual bands did their own bargaining, sometimes selling land that did not belong to them. U.S. Indian agents sometimes picked out chiefs who did not have the authority to sign treaties or speak for tribal members. Non-Indian settlers steadily moved in and stayed.

In an 1821 treaty, federal negotiators pressured the Potawatomi into giving up nearly all of southern Michigan and a strip of land around the south end of Lake Michigan, including Chicago and Milwaukee. Can you guess what this land is worth today? By 1829, the tribe had ceded about seventy percent (nearly three-fourths!) of its original land base.

One of the reasons that the Potawatomi had to sell their land was that the tribe had become poor. The Potawatomi had become increasingly dependent upon European trade goods. They were also used to getting French **credit**, which allowed them to run up large **debts** in the winter and pay them back with pelts in the spring. But hunting on less land meant fewer furs to trade. Non-Indian farms and fences now cut across on the landscape. The Potawatomi built up large debts, and non-Indians were happy to be paid back with land.

In the late 1820s, greed and fear led Americans to push the Potawatomi from the last of their homelands. Non-Indian lead miners had overrun southwestern Wisconsin and northern Illinois, settling on lands claimed by the Ho-Chunk, Potawatomi, and other Indians. Do you remember reading about Red Bird, the Ho-Chunk war chief in Chapter 4? The Potawatomi did not join the raids conducted by Red Bird. But the government took the Red Bird raids as a reason to force the Potawatomi to give up its lands in the lead district.

Then in 1830, President Andrew Jackson signed the Indian Removal Act. In this law, the United States claimed to have the authority to move *all* Indians living *east* of the Mississippi River to lands *west* of the river. Just three years later, in the Treaty of Chicago, the Potawatomi signed away the last of their lands east of the Mississippi River. By this time, the different Potawatomi bands had chosen different paths. Members of one band became

President Andrew Jackson

credit: Time allowed to pay money owed someone ◆ **debts:** Amounts of money owed

Christians, fought removal, and were allowed to remain in their village in Michigan. Another large group of Potawatomi from southeastern Wisconsin and northern Illinois unhappily agreed to move. But instead of heading west, they fled North to Canada. The bands from northeastern Wisconsin, however, refused to leave their homelands.

Dealing with Non-Indians

After the Treaty of Chicago, some Potawatomi people returned to their villages along Lake Michigan and lived peacefully for many years. But in 1862, an Indian revolt in Minnesota sparked panic among non-Indian settlers in Wisconsin. The settlers turned against *all* Indians. Some Potawatomi families moved farther north or hid in the forests. Without land of their own, they became known as the "Strolling Bands of Potawatomi."

For the Potawatomi who were forced west, the trip became known as the "Trail of Death." According to oral history, Potawatomi warriors were placed in chains and leg irons, crammed in wagons, and denied food and water until the end of each day's march. Any tribal member caught trying to give food or water to the warriors was severely punished. A small number managed to escape to Mexico, where they lived among the Kickapoo.

Along with the pressure to give up land, the Potawatomi also faced pressure to give up their traditional customs and religions. Treaties between the Potawatomi Nation and the U.S. government often called for the construction of mission schools and churches. The federal government thought that Christian leaders and educators were necessary to make the Potawatomi turn away from their Indian ways.

Potawatomi Removals

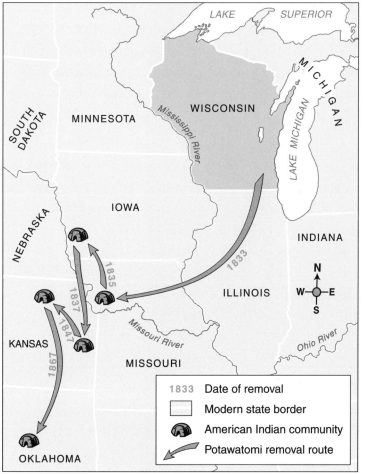

Map by Amelia Janes, Midwest Educational Graphics

Like other Native peoples in Wisconsin, Potawatomi children were often sent to boarding schools, where officials would not let them speak their language. Often the children could not practice their customs and religions. The Potawatomi responded to these pressures in different ways. Many accepted Christianity. Others mixed Christian beliefs with their own beliefs. Some Potawatomi escaped to northern forests, creating settlements where they could secretly practice their own religion, customs, and traditions.

By the beginning of the 1900s, the Potawatomi were scattered across seven states. The Strolling Bands in northeastern Wisconsin were especially **isolated** and poor. Because they refused to move west, the U.S. government

isolated: Kept separated or separate from others

105

would not give them land and the yearly amounts of money promised by treaty. Potawatomi women worked in the homes of non-Indian families. Potawatomi men found work as day laborers or lumberjacks. Entire families sometimes hired themselves out as **migrant** (**my** grunt) workers, picking potatoes and berries for white farmers and **canneries**. A few eventually managed to save enough to buy back bits of their homeland and homestead, but most Potawatomi people did not have enough money.

Location of Forest County

FOREST COUNTY

N
W—E
S

Map by Amelia Janes,
Midwest Educational Graphics

In 1909, a group of 457 Potawatomi was living in Forest County in northeastern Wisconsin. Despite the loss of land and the pressures to accept non-Indian ways, this Strolling Band of Potawatomi had never lost its tribal organization, its language, or its tribal identity. When U.S. senators visited Forest County, Chief **Kish-ki-kaam** (**keesh** key kahm) told them that his people wanted land together and wanted the land placed in trust "so that nobody can get it away from you." The Potawatomi had seen how other Indians had lost their land when it was allotted and taxed.

But the Potawatomi were not allowed to buy a large block of land, only scattered parcels. Their tribal lands in Forest County looked like a checkerboard, with some plots of land miles away from others. Most of this land was rocky and had already been logged,

migrant: People who move from place to place following available work ◆ **canneries:** Factories where foods are canned

leaving only the stumps of trees among the rocks. It was not good for farming. In 1913, these Strolling Potawatomi officially became the Forest County Potawatomi Community. The tribe bought reservation land between Crandon and Waubeno in Forest County with money promised in the 1833 treaty.

As you've learned in earlier chapters, in 1934 the Indian Reorganization Act (IRA) allowed the tribes to reorganize their tribal governments to be like town governments in the U.S. With the adoption of a tribal constitution, the Potawatomi at last owned a **refuge** (**ref** yooj) in their traditional homeland. The tribal population began to grow steadily as other Potawatomi moved to the reservation.

The 1940s and 1950s brought great changes to the Potawatomi. Some people did very well and made enough money to live more comfortably. With the coming of World War II in the early 1940s, many Potawatomi men volunteered for military service and left Wisconsin for the first time. A few

SKUNK HILL

In the early part of the 1900s, some Potawatomi families lived on Skunk Hill, located in Wood County in central Wisconsin. Today many Native people recognize it as a ceremonial site, burial ground, and a place to gather traditional medicines. Although only a few Potawatomi live in the region, Skunk Hill remains a very important place for the Potawatomi people.

WHS Archives, WHi(X3)47230

Potawatomi at Skunk Hill in Wood County, 1930

Photo courtesy of Potawatomi Travelling Times

Skunk Hill 2000

Location of Skunk Hill

Skunk Hill

Mississippi River

Wisconsin River

N
W E
S

Map by Amelia Janes, Midwest Educational Graphics

Potawatomi women moved to Milwaukee and other large cities to take jobs in the defense industry. The **migration** (my **gray** shun) to the cities continued after World War II.

In the 1950s, when the U.S. government adopted its "termination and relocation" policy, many Potawatomi members moved to cities. They were supposed to get government job training and housing assistance but many received only a one-way bus ticket to Milwaukee or Chicago and directions to run-down housing. Does this story of relocation remind you of similar promises made and broken to Ojibwe and Menominee tribal members?

Still, the Potawatomi adapted to these changes in their lives. Many worked in the cities during the week and returned home to the reservation on the weekends. These urban Potawatomi members formed relationships with other urban Indians and, in their own way, re-created clan and family ties. During the 1960s, they raised their voices and

migration: Movement from one community to another in the same country

demanded that government officials do something about the **poverty** (**pah** ver tee), bad housing, and the poor schools on the reservation and in the cities.

The 1970s remained difficult years for the Potawatomi people. Finally in 1988, the federal government granted the Forest County Band of Potawatomi reservation status.

Potawatomi Life Today

Gaming has really helped the Potawatomi economically. In the late 1980s, the tribe signed an agreement with the State of Wisconsin. The agreement established a casino between Waubeno and Carter in Forest County, and a bingo hall on its ancestral lands in the heart of Milwaukee. Eventually the bingo hall expanded into a casino. The casino has made a lot of money for the tribe. For the first time in several hundred years, the Potawatomi people have been able to build a foundation for the future. The tribe constructed a hotel and conference center next to its casino in Carter. Now the tribe also has other businesses, such as a construction company, a logging cooperative, a

Potawatomi casino in Milwaukee

poverty: Being very poor

convenience store, and a gas station. The Potawatomi recently established a red deer herd to provide venison to restaurants and other places.

The Potawatomi also give money to support the Indian School of Milwaukee. Open to children of all Indian nations, the school provides a strong general course of study. The school also builds pride and respect for traditional tribal values, such as respecting elders and caring for the environment. The tribe gives money to educational programs on reservations as well.

The Potawatomi's health and wellness center provides medical, dental, and mental health care. Other programs include a daycare center, a senior center, and services to the elderly, such as transportation, housing, home repair, and home-delivered meals. The tribe also operates a housing program for tribal members and a newspaper, *The Potawatomi Traveling Times.*

Marge Stevens, an Oneida parent volunteer, teaches a class at the Indian Community School of Milwaukee, Inc., 1971.

WHS Archives, WHI(X3)35353

The Potawatomi Nation hopes to provide services that continue to improve the lives of its 1,000 members, half of whom live on the reservation. The tribe wants to improve housing for all tribal members and find jobs for all those who are able to work. The Potawatomi Nation has also created an environmental department in order to improve and protect its landscape.

Remembering

The Potawatomi people continue to grow stronger. In 1998, the Potawatomi Nation shared its gaming revenues with another tribe—the Red Cliff Ojibwe. Although the Red Cliff Band has a casino, it does not make as much money as casinos closer to large cities. The Red Cliff Band has struggled to provide for its members. In their success, the Potawatomi have not forgotten the ancient responsibilities that tie them to their *Neshnabek* family. Helping the Red Cliff Ojibwe is one of the ways that "Bodewadmi"—Little Brother—continues to be "Keepers of the Fire."

The Oneida Nation

◆ ◆ ◆

The long history of the Oneida Nation began in what is now New York State, but has continued in Wisconsin for nearly two hundred years. When Europeans met them, the Oneida people occupied an area of about six million acres in New York. The Oneida were part of the Five Nations Confederacy (chapters 2 and 6). The other four were the Seneca, Cayuga, Onondaga and Mohawk Nations. They called themselves, the **Haudenosaunee** (ho dun a **show** nee), which means "People of the Long House." During the fur trade era, the Haudenosaunee may have been the most powerful group in North America!

Their oral tradition describes how the Haudenosaunee often fought with each other before they formed the confederacy. Speaking with the aid of his assistant, **Hiawatha** (hi ah **wah** tha), the Great Peacemaker visited Haudenosaunee villages and delivered the Great Law of Peace: "Together you are like the five fingers of a warrior's hand," he told them. "United you are powerful; divided you are weak." According to Oneida oral history, the Five Nations founded their Confederacy long before Europeans arrived in North America. The Great Peacemaker's wisdom proved correct. While the Five Nations stayed united, they were stronger than their enemies.

Oneida Long House

Think about It

What was life like for the Oneida when the tribe was part of the Five Nations Confederacy? Why did the tribe leave New York? How did the Oneida get to Wisconsin? What is the history of the Oneida since they arrived in our state?

Tribal Traditions

According to Oneida oral tradition, the world began in the Sky World after the Tree of Life was uprooted. This left a big hole between the sky and the watery world below it. Sky Woman fell into the hole, but as she fell, she managed to grab a twig from the Tree. Four white swans carried her safely to the watery world. Muskrat dived in to retrieve some earth. Turtle then offered his back as a place to put the earth, and this is where the spreading world was held. With seeds from the Tree of Life, Sky Woman began to plant and create Mother Earth.

The Oneida refer to themselves as the **Onyoteaka** (own yo day a gah) meaning "People of the Standing Stone." Oral tradition tells us that the name comes from the Oneida custom of moving villages every so often. At each new location, they placed a large, upright stone.

The Oneida were mostly farmers who raised corn, beans, and squash using a "slash and burn" method. Slashing and burning means burning off the ground cover, planting crops, and then moving the fields when the land no longer produces

Photo courtesy of Milwaukee Public Museum

Oneida boys took a break from picking berries while on a boarding school outing. How would you like to pick berries in a uniform?

well. The women made decisions about the land, worked the fields, and gathered roots, berries, and nuts. The men supplied game and fish. The Oneida also "deer-farmed" by burning underbrush, and sometimes the trees themselves, to create good habitats for deer. When the firewood was gone or the garden soil was used up, the Oneida moved. At other times, they relocated their villages when necessary for defense or to avoid European diseases.

A typical Haudenosaunee village contained dozens of Long Houses surrounded by a **palisade** (pal ih **sade**). The people built their houses of tall young trees; they tied the trees into an arch and covered them with sheets of elm bark. These houses ranged in size from forty feet long to two hundred feet long, which is more half the length of a football field!

A Long House provided a home for extended family members, who were related through the mother. Above the door of the Long House, the family painted its clan symbol, which might be a wolf, a bear, or a turtle. A man marrying an Oneida woman would move into his bride's Long House, and their children would become members of her clan.

Tribal History

Meeting Europeans in New York

By the 1800s, the Oneida lived in large villages, mostly in present-day New York and Pennsylvania. The first Oneida meeting with Europeans was not a friendly one. It happened in 1615, when the Samuel de **Champlain** (sham **plain**), the Frenchman who had established Quebec, Canada, raided an Oneida village. During a

---

palisade: A large fence for protection

three-hour battle, Champlain's men set fire to the village and killed many of its defenders. Champlain's attack was frightening, but European diseases were even worse. Almost half of the Oneida population died from smallpox, influenza, and measles.

Like other Haudenosaunee communities, the Oneida traded furs, first with the Dutch and later with the British. The Oneida competed against the French and their Indian allies, who were mainly Algonquian nations, such as the Ojibwe, Potawatomi, and Huron Nations.

By 1649, the Haudenosaunee had become very powerful. They strongly influenced other Indian nations across much of eastern North America. Tribes who wished to participate in the Haudenosaunee trade network could do so only with the permission and protection of one of the original Five Nations.

WHO LED THE FIVE NATIONS CONFEDERACY?

The Five Nations Confederacy was governed by a Grand Council made up of fifty leaders, chosen by the clan mothers. The Grand Council included representatives from each tribe. The leaders, who were selected based on their qualities of honesty and integrity, guided the Five Nations during times of peace and conflict. When the Haudenosaunee faced outside threats, war chiefs assumed certain responsibilities. Although all Five Nations belonged to the confederacy, each nation was free to act alone, which it did from time to time.

After the Haudenosaunee had defeated the Huron, they adopted many Huron people into the tribe. The Haudenosaunee then turned their attention to their competitors in the fur trade, including the Anishinaabe. When the Anishinaabe tried to take furs by canoe up the St. Lawrence River to Quebec for trade, the Haudenosaunee warriors got mad. The Haudenosaunee often sent large war parties into the Great Lakes to stop this trade, but they were not always successful.

Occasionally the Haudenosaunee nations disagreed with each other, especially after Christian missionaries arrived. In 1667, the Jesuits persuaded a few Christian Oneida families to settle near their mission in the St. Lawrence Valley. The soil was not good for corn, so the families moved to a new village, **Kahnawake** (gon ah **wah** gay). At the beginning, only Oneida families lived in the village, but later more and more Christian Mohawk families joined them.

The Oneida and the American Revolution

By the year 1775, the Haudenosaunee were worried about the growing troubles between England and the American colonies. So, they sent representatives to meet with several American officials. The Americans asked the Haudenosaunee to be neutral in the coming American Revolution. By now, the Haudenosaunee had expanded in number. When the **Tuscarora** (tus kuh **ror** uh) joined the Haudenosaunee, they became known as

POLLY COOPER STORY

Polly Cooper, an Oneida woman, cooked for Washington and his staff when they stayed in Philadelphia. Cooper knew that the Americans were running short of money, and so she told them not to pay her. While window-shopping one day, Polly and Washington's wife, Martha, saw a shawl that Polly admired. As a thank you, the **Continental Congress** (kon tuh nen **tl** kon gruhs) voted to buy the shawl for her. The gift has been passed down from generation to generation and is still owned by members of the Oneida Nation.

Polly Cooper

Image courtesy of the Oneida Indian Nation of New York

the Six Nations Confederacy. The Six Nations had differing opinions about the American Revolution. Some tribes supported the British. The Oneida and some Tuscarora members a served as scouts, runners, and spies for the Americans. Still others were neutral.

In 1777, the Oneida and smaller numbers of Tuscarora and Mohawk helped the Americans. These three tribes played an important role in the war, helping in a number of major battles. During the winter of 1777, at Valley Forge, the Oneida supplied George Washington's troops with six hundred bushels of corn and other food items that the American troops needed.

Despite their loyalty during the American Revolution, the Oneida faced hostile American neighbors and dishonest developers after the war. In 1785 and again in 1788, New York officials forced the Oneida into a series of leases and treaties that cheated the tribe out of more than 5.5 million acres of land.

IROQUOIS INFLUENCE ON THE U.S. CONSTITUTION AND GOVERNMENT

The members of the Continental Congress created the U.S. Constitution and our form of government. Benjamin Franklin and others drew upon some good ideas that already existed. Some were from Europe. Some were from the Iroquois constitution, known as The Great Law of Peace. The Great Law of Peace expressed the Iroquois political ideas. The new ideas from The Great Law of Peace included thinking of leaders as servants of the people and making rules to punish leaders for bad behavior. Iroquois law and custom supported freedom of expression, political participation by women, and sharing of wealth.

During this stressful time, Eleazar Williams arrived and began planning to move some Oneida families westward. He became an Episcopal Church missionary to the

Haudenosaunee. Within a few years, Williams began making plans for a "Grand **Iroquois** (**ear** uh kwoy) Empire" of Lake Michigan. He began negotiating a land purchase from the Menominee and Ho-Chunk Nations.

Eleazar Williams
WHS Archives, WHi(X28)1078

Moving to Wisconsin

In 1821, Williams traveled with a group of Oneida and other New York Indians to Green Bay. He asked for a strip of land along the Fox River north of Lake Winnebago. Under pressure from the United States government, the Menominee and Ho-Chunk agreed. The following year, Williams returned with a larger group and wanted to expand the land purchase to six million acres!

The Menominee Nation, the Oneida Nation, and the U.S. government have different stories about what happened. The U.S. government said that the Menominee sold the land. The Menominee and Oneida people understood that they had agreed upon joint use, or sharing of the land. The Ho-Chunk refused to participate in the discussion.

WHS Archives, WHi(X3)40387

Oneida Civil War veterans pose for a picture around 1907.

119

Early Years in Wisconsin

In 1824, around one hundred members of the Oneida Nation and an equal number of Mohicans, settled along the Fox River. The following year, another 150 families joined them. They created a permanent settlement at Duck

Oneida Migration from New York to Wisconsin

Map by Amelia Janes, Midwest Educational Graphics

Creek, west of Green Bay. However, not all of the Oneida approved of migrating west.

But many Oneida members believed that their only chance for survival was in the west. By 1838, more than six hundred and fifty members of the tribe were living at Duck Creek, where they planted fields of corn, potatoes, and turnips.

That year, the Oneida groups negotiated a treaty with the United States that officially established their reservation boundaries. One hundred acres of land were set aside for each tribal member. The land was to be held in common, that is, the people would own it together. But the Oneida people who moved from New York to Wisconsin after 1838 did not have a share in the ownership of the reservation. These members of the Oneida Nation were known as the "Homeless Band." They had no land until 1891.

120

In the 1840s and 1850s, many European immigrants arrived in the Green Bay area. This placed new pressures on the tribe. During the American Civil War (1861-1865), the Oneida people experienced more hard times: long **droughts** (drowts), early frosts, and outbreaks of smallpox. One hundred thirty-five Oneida men—about ten percent of the total Oneida population—volunteered for duty with the Union Army. But they paid a terrible price. Only fifty-five of the volunteers returned from the war!

Allotment of Oneida lands began in 1891. The results, as elsewhere in Indian Country, were a nightmare. Many Oneida members did not understand American government's system of taxation. They lost their lands when they failed to pay their taxes. Others were tricked by dishonest land companies. By the 1930s, less than five percent of the original Oneida Reservation remained in the hands of tribal members.

The Indian Reorganization Act ended allotment and required the Oneida to reorganize their tribal government to be more like that of the United States. Only then did the U.S. officials buy back nearly 1,300 acres and place it in trust for the Oneida Nation.

The educational experience for Oneida children was a mixed one. Most Oneida children went to either the Christian boarding school or the government boarding school on the reservation. Other children went away to schools in Pennsylvania or Virginia. Both the church schools and the government schools only allowed students to speak English. Schools also discouraged any expression of Oneida language and culture.

droughts: Long periods of dry weather when little or no rain falls

Photo courtesy of Milwaukee Public Museum

Girls in the Oneida Indian School laundry room. How would you like to study "laundry?"

Many parents wished to protect their children from the harsh treatment they had been through. So, they encouraged their children to adopt non-Indian ways. As one tribal member sadly explained, "My mother and father both spoke Oneida, but [not so much] in front of us kids." As a result, fewer people spoke Oneida, and they could only practice Oneida traditions secretly.

MILITARY MEN AND PATRIOTIC WOMEN

During World War I, one hundred fifty Oneida men were among ten thousand Indians who volunteered for active duty, even though many were not even U.S. citizens. In World War II, more than seventy percent of Oneida men enlisted and more than two hundred were killed. Do you remember reading about Ojibwe "code-talkers" in chapter 5? Oneida men were also part of the U.S. Army's 32nd Infantry Division. They, too, used their language to keep military secrets from the Japanese. Oneida women supported the war effort by buying war bonds, and they moved to cities and took jobs in factories making equipment that soldiers needed. A few Oneida women even joined the military.

Giving up their traditional ways also led to a scattering of the Oneida people. Although some tribal members found jobs in the non-Indian communities that now surrounded them, many of the best-educated Oneida moved off the reservation to find jobs. Many have returned now that jobs are available on the reservation.

In the 1940s and 1950s, members of the Oneida Nation continued to move to urban areas, particularly Milwaukee, to find work. But they found what other relocated Indians experienced: poor housing, poor jobs, and separation from their culture. However, under the leadership of several Oneida, the Indian community in the city became a home away from home—a kind of urban reservation.

Kim Cornelius-Nishimoto works on her cornhusk dolls.

Finished cornhusk dolls

Oneida Life Today

The 1980s brought positive changes for the Oneida Nation. The Oneida Nation was one of the first Indian tribes to sign a gaming agreement with the State of Wisconsin. The gaming agreement allowed the tribe to set up a casino on the reservation near Green Bay. The Oneida Nation then used casino dollars to help the tribe create other businesses. Today the Oneida Nation owns other businesses, including convenience stores, a large organic farm, an electronics firm, and a business park in Brown County. With casino dollars, the Oneida Nation has bought back thousands of acres of its original reservation.

In addition to its successful businesses, the tribe operates a public museum and library. The tribe also provides health services, housing, and almost one hundred other programs for its members. One of its greatest successes is the Oneida Tribal School. The tribe built the school in the shape of a turtle to remember Sky Woman and the Haudenosaunee creation story. The Oneida Nation also offers early childhood, Head Start, high school, and higher education opportunities to its tribal members.

Photo courtesy of Oneida Nation

Aerial view of the Oneida Tribal School, built in the shape of a turtle.

Remembering

The U.S. government is slowly reversing the two-hundred-year-old wrongs done to the Oneida Nation. In 1985, the U.S. Supreme Court ruled that New York state officials had acted illegally in taking two hundred seventy thousand acres of Oneida land in New York. The state eventually will have to repay the tribe for this wrong. In the meantime, conditions for the Oneida people in Wisconsin continue to improve as tribal businesses make more money, provide people with better opportunities, and help tribal members reclaim their traditional Haudenosaunee values.

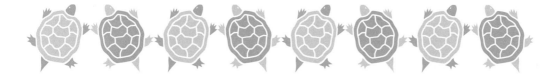

Chapter 8

The Mohican Nation, Stockbridge-Munsee Band and the Brothertown Indians

◆ ◆ ◆

Muh-he-con-nuk (mo **he** cuh nuk), the name Mohicans give themselves, means "The People of the Waters That Are Never Still." These are the tribal waters of the Atlantic Ocean in present-day New York. The tribe settled along the banks of the Hudson and lower Housatonic rivers from Lake Champlain to Manhattan. The original Mohican homeland lay in the far north and west. According to Mohican oral history, the tribe made their way to the Atlantic.

When Mohican people first met Europeans in the 1600s, the tribe was living along the Hudson River near Lake Champlain. The Dutch called the tribe, *Mahican,* a shorter version of Muh-he-con-nuk. The Mohicans spoke an Algonquian language. Like the Oneida, both the Mohican Nation Stockbridge-Munsee Band and the Brothertown Indians journeyed west to Wisconsin in the 1820s and have been here ever since.

Think about It

Why did the Mohicans move from New York to Wisconsin? Where are Mohican people in Wisconsin today? Where does the name Stockbridge-Munsee Band come from? Who are the Brothertown Indians? Where do they come from? Where in Wisconsin do the Brothertown Indians live today? How do they fit into this chapter with the Mohicans? The stories of these two tribes are different, but they made Wisconsin their home about the same time.

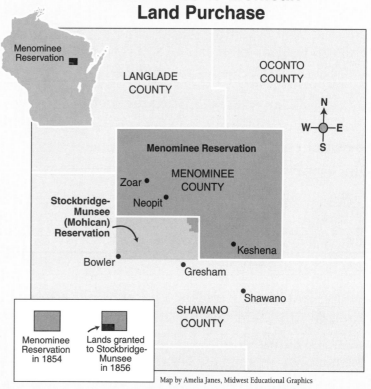

Menominee to Mohican Land Purchase

Menominee Reservation

LANGLADE COUNTY

OCONTO COUNTY

Menominee Reservation

MENOMINEE COUNTY

Zoar

Stockbridge-Munsee (Mohican) Reservation

Neopit

Keshena

Bowler

Gresham

Shawano

SHAWANO COUNTY

Menominee Reservation in 1854

Lands granted to Stockbridge-Munsee in 1856

Map by Amelia Janes, Midwest Educational Graphics

127

Mohican Tribal Traditions

The Mohicans had as many as forty villages in New York, Massachusetts, Connecticut, and Vermont. Each village contained about two hundred people. The Mohican villages were protected by palisades. Inside the walls, tribal members lived in wigwams or Long Houses, which sheltered several families of the same clan. The Mohican people were hunters, fishers, gatherers, and gardeners who planted corn, beans, and squash together with sunflowers. Women did the gardening; men provided fish and game. The Mohicans moved their villages as often as necessary in order to be near fresh garden soil.

Mohican towns were headed by leaders known as **sachems** (**sa** chums). A council of clan leaders directed the sachems. The most important clans were the Bear, Wolf, Turkey and Turtle. Sachems met regularly in the main village of Shodac, which is east of present-day Albany, the capital of New York. In times of war, the tribe passed leadership to a war chief.

Tribal History

When Europeans first arrived in the New York, the Mohicans had about a thousand warriors out of their total population of twenty thousand. Because the Mohicans were eager to trade, word spread that the Mohicans were willing and friendly traders. Like all of the tribes of the Great Lakes and New England, the Mohicans adapted quickly to the fur trade and started using European trade items, which included guns, copper kettles, scissors, and liquor. Throughout the next few years many Dutch settlers moved into Mohican territory to trade furs and take land. Through trade, the Mohicans were strong allies of the Dutch.

sachems: Tribal leaders

The Mohicans' conflicts with the Mohawks and increasing numbers of Dutch and French pushed the Mohicans from their homeland. By 1724, the Mohicans had only two villages in present-day Massachusetts. European diseases took a deadly toll on the tribe's population, which dropped to less than a thousand people.

The Mohicans of Stockbridge, Massachusetts

The Mohicans began to listen to the messages of missionaries who had come to their villages. As a result, many tribal members became Christians. In 1734, the Mohicans agreed to host a mission in a village they called "the Great Meadow," known to the Europeans as "Stockbridge." Within a few years, several hundred Christian Indians also settled there. American settlers did not notice the distinct tribal identities of the Indians who lived in Stockbridge, and called them simply the Stockbridge Indians.

During this time, the Mohicans' culture began to change. Surrounded now by fences and property lines, the Mohicans could no longer pick up and move when their garden soil was used up, as had been their tradition. Tribal members adapted to this change and borrowed farming methods from their non-Indian neighbors. Some worked as farmhands, lumberjacks, or on whalers and fishing ships. Others developed skills, like carpentry. Mohican women moved through the countryside, selling handmade baskets, wooden bowls, brooms, and moccasins.

Mohican culture absorbed non-Indian culture. Most tribal members replaced wigwams with frame houses and wore clothes made of cloth rather than buckskin. As Christians, Mohicans worshipped in churches and sent their children to non-Indian schools.

More Europeans arived. These new settlers pushed the Mohicans from their homes and farms. British officials promised to help return the lost land to the Mohicans, but nothing came of it.

The Mohicans entered the American Revolution on the side of the Americans. They fought and served as scouts in many battles. The tribe's losses during the war were terrible. Half of all Mohican fighting men were killed. Monuments to their bravery are on three battlefields.

Mohicans Meet the Brothertown Indians

The Mohican people began to look for a new home. When the Oneida invited them to live in their nation, the Mohicans accepted. In the mid-1780s, the Mohicans packed up and resettled near Oneida Lake in upstate New York. The Mohicans settled on land that the Oneida gave them as their sovereign home. The Mohicans lived next to land that the Oneida had given another group of Algonquian Nations. Their settlement was known as Brothertown. People living there became known as Brothertown Indians. The Brothertown did well until a series of bad treaties and illegal land leases forced the tribe to move.

In 1818, two groups of Mohicans led by John **Metoxin** (meh **tox** sin) and Joseph Quinney left New York. One group traveled to present-day

Indiana to live among their friends and relatives, the Delaware Munsee. The trip was long. By the time the Mohican groups arrived in Indiana, the Delaware Munsee had been forced to sell their land. Now the Delaware Munsee were preparing for removal to lands in southwestern Missouri.

Many Trails to Wisconsin: Mohicans of Stockbridge, the Munsee and the Brothertown

In 1821, the first group of Mohicans of Stockbridge traveled to the Upper Great Lakes region. Between 1822 and 1829, groups of Mohican, Munsee, and Brothertown Indians arrived in what is today east-central Wisconsin. The first Mohican arrivals settled at Grand Cackalin (known today as Kaukauna), on the Fox River. But disputes over the land sale led to new treaty negotiations. In 1834, the Mohicans moved to two townships of land along the eastern shore of Lake Winnebago. They called their settlement "Brothertown." Known first as the Stockbridge and Munsee people, their community was later called the "Stockbridge-Munsee" community.

In a treaty negotiated in 1838, the government promised all the "New York" Indians land in Kansas. In 1839, the Mohican Nation sold one township. Some members joined a group of Munsee from Canada who were moving to Indian County west of the Mississippi in what is now Kansas. Many died in Kansas from heat and disease, but some struggled back to Wisconsin. Some remained in Kansas and are still there.

Stockbridge-Munsee and the Brothertown Leaving New York

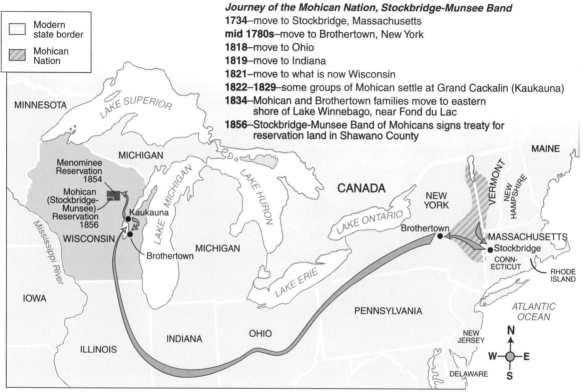

Legend:
- Modern state border
- Mohican Nation

Journey of the Mohican Nation, Stockbridge-Munsee Band

1734—move to Stockbridge, Massachusetts
mid 1780s—move to Brothertown, New York
1818—move to Ohio
1819—move to Indiana
1821—move to what is now Wisconsin
1822–1829—some groups of Mohican settle at Grand Cackalin (Kaukauna)
1834—Mohican and Brothertown families move to eastern shore of Lake Winnebago, near Fond du Lac
1856—Stockbridge-Munsee Band of Mohicans signs treaty for reservation land in Shawano County

Map by Amelia Janes, Midwest Educational Graphics

The Mohicans' problems continued throughout the next ten years. In 1843, Congress offered U.S. citizenship to the Mohicans. Some Mohicans became citizens and sold their lands to non-Indian developers, or they lost their property when they did not pay their taxes. Others, including John W. Quinney refused to cooperate with

WHS Archives, WHi(X3)45435

John W. Quinney

those who wanted Mohican land. Under Quinney's leadership, the Mohicans fought efforts to remove the tribe and take their land. In 1856, the Mohicans negotiated the last of their treaties. This resulted in another move, this time to the southwest corner of the Menominee Reservation.

The Brothertown People in Wisconsin

At first, the Brothertown Indians did well in Wisconsin, but soon they faced increasing pressure from non-Indian settlers. Believing it was the best way to keep their land, the Brothertown accepted U.S. citizenship in 1839. Congress passed legislation that changed their reservation to a town and divided the tribe's land holdings into private property that was allotted to each tribal member. In the eyes of the United States, the government of the Brothertown Indians no longer existed.

As it had done with the other tribes in Wisconsin, allotment ended in disaster. The Brothertown quickly lost their lands when they could not pay necessary taxes. By 1880, many were living with friends and relatives on the Oneida and Mohican Reservations. If they were lucky, they worked as day laborers in neighboring non-Indian communities. Yet, the Brothertown continued to function as a tribe. They sent formal letters to Congress and joined a lawsuit with other New York tribes over treaty matters. In 1878, Congress asked for the tribe's advice about the sale of some Brothertown land. A hundred years later, in a struggle to restore tribal status, the Brothertown argued that these government-to-government negotiations showed that the federal government recognized the Brothertown as a tribe.

The Mohicans, the Brothertown, and the U.S. Government

The years following allotment (1887—1934) were very difficult for both the Mohicans and the Brothertown Indians. Timber companies clear-cut the tribes' pine forests, leaving the land in terrible condition. Much of the land had thin and sandy soil that was not suitable for farming, and the growing season was too short. People were no longer able to make a living from logging the land and had trouble feeding their families. By 1934, less than half of the original Mohican Reservation remained in tribal hands.

The Mohicans also lost their most precious resource—their children. The U.S. government forced Mohicans, like other Indian nations, to send their children to boarding schools. There the educators refused to let students use their traditional language or practice their traditional cultural expression. "They tried to erase us," explained Dorothy Davids, who attended the Lutheran Mission School in Red Springs. "They tried to make us into something else." Davids described herself as one of the luckier children. Every Friday afternoon, her grandfather came to the mission to pick her up

FIRST WISCONSIN WOMAN TO TEACH PUBLIC SCHOOL

Electa Quinney

Photo courtesy of Electa Quinney Elementary School, Kaukauna

John Quinney's sister, Electa, became the first female public schoolteacher in the state. Born into the Mohican tribe in 1802, Electa Quinney was educated in mission schools in Connecticut and New York. She taught school in New York before her family, along with her tribe, left for Wisconsin. In 1827, the tribe built a church and a log schoolhouse. It was a free school, open to anyone of any denomination. A year later, Electa took over the classroom and the tribe paid her salary. In a letter to friends back east, she expressed her hope for the Mohicans in Wisconsin when she told friends, "The people have much improved since leaving New York." And the minister said that she taught as well as any man.

and take her home for the weekend. Other children stayed at the mission for the entire school year, returning home only in the summers, if at all. Some Mohican children attended Indian boarding schools in Wisconsin communities like Gresham and Tomah, but a few were sent as far away as South Dakota and Pennsylvania.

The experiences of Mohican children at the mission school were mixed. Dorothy Davids' sister, Bernice Miller Pigeon, recalled her years as happy ones. Like Davids, Pigeon was able to return to her family each weekend. Davids described the school as "not bad" but a place where punishment could be harsh. Davids became the first American Indian woman to graduate from the University of Wisconsin—Stevens Point and later earned a master's degree at the University of Wisconsin—Milwaukee. She believes that what the Indian children learned proved useful, "by getting some skills, later we were able to stand up and criticize some of the government's policies."

And, as you have been reading throughout the book, there was much to criticize. However, some of that did change with passage of the Indian Reorganization Act in 1934. Federal officials began closing the boarding schools and buying back tribal land lost through allotment. The government returned fifteen thousand acres of land to the Mohicans, which allowed them to rebuild their community. In 1938, the Mohicans reorganized their tribal government and approved a new constitution.

Like other Indian people, many Mohicans moved to the cities in the 1950s as part of the government's relocation program. By 1966, less than half the Mohicans listed on the tribal rolls lived on their reservation. Dorothy Davids saw the tragic effects of relocation at the American Indian Center in Chicago, "Native people losing their jobs . . . and having a hard time adjusting to urban life."

Urban Indian centers, such as the one in Chicago worked quietly to help people. But in the 1960s and 1970s, the American Indian Movement (AIM) protested loudly and frightened many non-Indians. But AIM focused national attention on problems facing Native people, such as poor health care and poverty. "Without AIM, a lot of the changes wouldn't have occurred," Davids said, "All we had to say was, 'I guess we'll just have to call in AIM,' and we usually got what we wanted. It was an exciting time."

The Mohican Nation, Stockbridge-Munsee Band Today

The Mohican people who left Stockbridge, New York, and journeyed with the Munsee people to Wisconsin, now call themselves the "Mohican Nation, Stockbridge-Munsee Band." The "Mohican Nation" part of their name honors their tribal government's relationship with non-Indian governments in Wisconsin and in Washington D.C. The "Stockbridge-Munsee Band" part of their name honors their history.

The arrival of gaming in the late 1980s brought better times for the Mohicans. In addition to a casino, the Mohican Nation, Stockbridge-Munsee Band owns a bingo hall, and operates a golf course, a campground, family and community centers, senior citizen housing, and the Arvid E. Miller Memorial Library Museum.

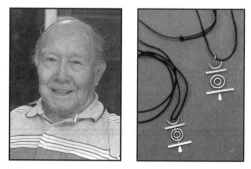

Edwin Martin and his jewelry featuring the Many Trails symbol

Edwin's photo by Lewis Koch for the Wisconsin Folk Museum Woodland Indian Project, courtesy of the UW-Madison Folklore Program; Jewelry photo by Rick March

136

The tribe also has dozens of tribal programs on their reservation, including Head Start and a health clinic. The Stockbridge-Munsee Band has also worked to add to the natural beauty of the reservation. The tribe recently improved Many Trails Park, adding picnic areas and footbridges. The tribe is the largest employer in Shawano County, and this adds to the economic development of the whole area.

Many Trails Park

Photo by Patty Loew

The Brothertown Indians Today

Meanwhile, the Brothertown Indian Tribe of Wisconsin does not exist "officially." In 1996, the Brothertown asked the U.S. government for formal recognition. They are still waiting for an answer. The Brothertown Tribal Council continues to meet monthly in Fond du Lac, and tribal members are optimistic that the U.S. government will soon recognize the Brothertown as an American Indian Nation.

Remembering

The Mohican Nation, Stockbridge-Munsee Band and the Brothertown Indians have separate stories that sometimes weave together on their journey to Wisconsin. With the tribe's promising businesses and community programs, Mohicans are returning to the reservation for jobs and opportunities. Such opportunities include cultural expression, such as pow wows. The "Many Trails" symbol can be seen on banners, jewelry, and T-shirts, reminding everyone of the difficult paths that mark Mohican history. But the "Many Trails" symbol also encourages tribal members to see possibilities in the journey that lies ahead.

Photo courtesy of Mohican News

Stockbridge-Munsee member Princess Storme Vele and Menominee member Danielle Kakwitch talk at a pow wow in Bowler, Wisconsin.

The Brothertown Indians see formal recognition by the U.S. government as an opportunity to make their own tribal identity stronger. "We want to preserve our heritage," says tribal chairperson June Ezold. "We want to do this for ourselves and our ancestors."

Native People of Wisconsin

◆ ◆ ◆

Menominee Nation

Keeping Traditions Alive: Dana Madosh and Brianna Ninham

Eleven-year-old Dana Madosh has an important goal: to preserve and protect his sacred Menominee language. Dana is a 6th grader at the Menominee Tribal School. Each day he delivers morning announcements in his Native language. He is often asked to do prayers for gatherings. Dana's family encourages him to practice traditional ways. These include attending pow wows, where he is a Grass Dancer. In 2002, Dana won the title, Menominee Tribal School Warrior. His goal is to become a fluent speaker and teacher of the Menominee language.

Tradition is also important to Brianna Ninham, who in 2002 was chosen Menominee Tribal School Princess. Brianna has served on the student council for four consecutive years. She has received the "Student of the Year" award and the "Okemawiakisaeh" award, which recognizes leadership. Brianna is a traditional dancer and member of the 5 Clan Singers, an alcohol and drug-free group. Because of her many accomplishments, Brianna was awarded Eagle Feathers, a high honor in the Menominee community.

Sharing Menominee Culture: Brooke Caldwell: 4th Grader

Like nearly half the Native American children in the United States, nine-year-old Brooke Caldwell, lives in a city, not on a reservation. Brooke's Menominee family lives near the University of Wisconsin-Madison, where her mother and father are going to school. Brooke's mom attends law school. Her father studies sustainable forestry. Brooke is in the fourth grade at Shorewood Elementary School where students at her school come from thirty different countries and speak fifty different languages. Brooke looks forward to International Day at the school, when she wears traditional Menominee dress and shares her culture with other students. For a science project, Brooke researched the traditional food dyes that the Menominee people used to color clothing.

Ho-Chunk Nation

Ho-Chunk Marathon Runner: Larry Garvin

When he crossed the finish line at the 2001 Honolulu Marathon, eighteen-year-old Ho-Chunk runner Larry Garvin, Jr., threw his hands in the air and shouted, "Yeah! Yeah!" Larry's time of three hours and fifty-six minutes was his personal best for the 26.2-mile race. He and the other eleven members of the Ho-Chunk Youth Marathon team had been training for three months, running 65 miles a week. Larry says marathon running helps build his confidence.

War Hero: Mitchell Red Cloud

In August 1941, at the age of sixteen, Mitchell Red Cloud joined the U.S. Marines. He was part of some of the heaviest fighting in the Pacific in World War II and was awarded two purple hearts for being wounded in battle. He went back to the Marines during the Korean War. During a battle there, he saw the enemy approaching and sounded the alarm. He fought them all by himself in order to give the rest of his company time to organize behind him for battle. He held his position until he was hit by enemy fire. Wounded, he pulled himself to his feet and wrapped his arm around a tree. He continued to fight until he received a wound that ended his life. Mitchell Red Cloud was a true hero and a great warrior for his country and all of its citizens.

Ojibwe Nation

Lacrosse Goalie: Alex Gokee

Zing! That's the sound a lacrosse ball makes when it whizzes into a goal on the Red Cliff Ojibwe Reservation. As a goalie for the Red Cliff Sugarbushers, it's thirteen-year-old Alex Gokee's job is to try and stop balls traveling about fifty miles an hour. During the summer and early fall, the Sugarbushers play other lacrosse teams from Oneida and Leech Lake.

Red Cliff youth lacrosse team

Native people invented lacrosse a long time ago. They have played it for fun, and sometimes, the have played it to settle arguments. "I think it's pretty cool because we

141

get to do the old traditions of our ancestors," Alex says. In the past, the Ojibwe used wooden sticks with a basket on the end. The sticks were about the size of a regular golf club. Today, Alex and others use an aluminum stick with a much bigger basket. Alex's grandfather was famous for carving the old style sticks and his uncle carries on the tradition. When Alex received one of the old-style sticks last summer, he was grateful, but said, "I don't know how anyone caught the ball with one of those."

Park Ranger: Katrina Werchouski

Katrina **Werchouski** (wer **chow** skee) is a member of the Red Cliff Band. She is the **valedictorian** (val uh dik **tor** e un) of the 2003 class of Bayfield High School and is attending the University fo Wisconsin-Stevens Point where she is studying natural resource management and environmental law enforcement. Katrina got interested in these subjects by growing up in Bayfield, where she recognized the beauty of the natural surroundings there and realized the need to protect them. In the summer of 1999, Katrina began to work for the National Park Service at the Apostle Islands National Lakeshore headquarters as part of a student school-to-work program. When she turned sixteen, she was old enough to work for as a park ranger for the National Park Service. Her job is to educate the visitors about the importance of National Park programs and of preserving the environment and natural resources.

· **valedictorian:** The graduating senior with the highest grades in the class

Potawatomi Nation

House Builder: Brad Shampo

When Brad Shampo finishes high school this year, he'll be able to say something few students can: "I built a house!" Brad is one of the Potawatomi students in a technology class that offers them hands-on experience in home building. The class is a cooperative effort between the Crandon School District and the Forest County Potawatomi Education and Housing Departments. Brad has learned roofing, carpentry, plumbing, and other skills of the construction trade. The house he and the others built will become the home of a Forest County Potawatomi tribal member.

Tae Kwon Do Yellow Belt: Ashley White

Twice a week you can find thirteen-year-old Ashley White, Potawatomi, in a gym punching, kicking, blocking, and breaking things. That may seem a bit unusual for someone whose sport is all about courtesy and self-control. But Ashley has a yellow belt in **Tae Kwon Do** (ty kwahn **do**), a martial art that came from Korea. Tae Kwon Do is a little like Karate, but it is for self-defense only. Ashley lives on the Potawatomi Reservation near Crandon. Tae Kwon Do gets Ashley in shape for another favorite activity: fancy dancing at pow wows. When she grows up, Ashley says she wants to be a lawyer.

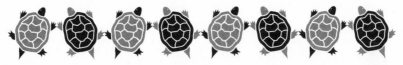

Oneida Nation

Oneida Hockey Players: John and Jayne Danforth

Almost any weekend, you can find the brother and sister team of John and Jayne Danforth on a sheet of ice somewhere in the Midwest. Eleven-year-old John is a defenseman for the Warcats, a peewee hockey team that plays at the Cornerstone Community Center rink in Green Bay, Wisconsin. Fifteen-year-old Jayne is goalie on her girls U-15 team, the Bobcats. John has been playing hockey since he was seven years old. Jayne started playing when she was eleven. Games involving balls and sticks have been played for thousands of years around the world. Did you know that when Europeans arrived in North America they found Native people playing a game very similar to hockey?

Oneida hockey players John and Jayne Danforth

Student Actress: Layni Stevens

Eleven-year-old Layni Stevens will always remember her 5th grade year at the Oneida Tribal School. That's the year she played Turtle in her school play, "The Turtle War Party." The play came from a story written in 1904 by the Oneida Chief Cornplanter. "The Turtle War Party" tells the story of how the animals react when humans intrude their territory. Like many Oneida stories, it delivers messages about greed, trust, and patience.

Left: Layni Stevens as a turtle in her school play. Right: Layni Stevens

144

Mohican Nation, Stockbridge-Munsee Nation

Musician: Bill Miller

Bill Miller grew up on the Stockbridge-Munsee Reservation. He graduated from nearby Shawano High School. Of his childhood, he recalls: "We didn't have much. There was nothing but woods, trout, and a Zenith radio that picked up AM stations across the country . . . I became a fan of all kinds of good music."

Bill Miller

Bill organized his first music group while attending the University of Wisconsin-La Crosse. He is a painter and sculptor, but he is best known as a singer, songwriter, guitarist, and as a player of the Native American flute. His music often deals with issues about the environment, Native history and traditions, and personal strength and courage.

At the 2000 Native American Music Awards, Bill received awards for Artist of the Year, Album of the Year, Songwriter of the Year, and Song of the Year. Yet Bill says: "My faith in my Creator leaves me content with the gifts I have, and I use them to enrich the world through His blessings."

Special Student: Gregg W. Duffek II

Born on July 26, 1987, Gregg W. Duffek II has two older and two younger **siblings**. The family lives onthe Stockbridge-Munsee Reservation. At birth, Gregg was diagnosed with a form of **cerebral palsy** (**seh** ruh bruhl **paul** zee) that affected his movements from the waist down. When Gregg was three years old, he started attending school in nearby Bowler.

---

siblings: Brothers and sisters ◆ **cerebral palsy:** Lack of control over some muscles, caused by brain damage before or during birth

145

He was happy to attend school and looked forward to it. The Bowler School, however, was not really prepared for students like Gregg. Common places like bathrooms had almost no handicap **access** (**ak** ses), making it difficult for anyone like Gregg who has special needs. Throughout many years at the school, Gregg loved to tell his grandmas and grandpas about the great things he learned at the school.

Gregg paved the way for other students with special needs. Over time, the school improved access. Although he is very independent, school staff and students help Gregg with every problem that comes up. Most times, he can be found surrounded by many friends or staff. At sixteen, Gregg has many accomplishments. He has a temporary driver's permit and is looking forward to obtaining his driver's license. School will always be a challenge for him, and making his way through unfriendly buildings and public places will continue to require him to speak up for changes.

Gregg has many careers in mind for his future. He likes to cook and bake, and he might be interested in his own TV cooking show, if he does not become a doctor or lawyer.

access: Ability to enter or use

Beyond

◆ ◆ ◆

By reading this book you have learned a lot about the Indian nations in Wisconsin. You have learned that they are indeed sovereign nations, communities of people with their own governments and their own laws. But you know now that the Indian citizens of these sovereign nations are also citizens of the United States.

Before reading this book, you may have thought that all Indians lived in teepees, wore feathers, and rode horses. Now you know that that is just not true. The twelve Indian nations in Wisconsin are alike in some ways, but in many ways they are very different.

Do you remember in which ways they are alike? All the nations signed treaties with the federal government. Most of them have reservations in Wisconsin. Nearly all of them experienced allotment, the division of their land. They all felt the effects of boarding schools and other assimilation programs. This was the government's effort to make them less Indian and more like their non-Indian neighbors.

By reading this book, you understand now that the Indian communities in Wisconsin are unique. They have different languages, different customs, and different cultures. Sometimes the Indian communities work together on programs that are important to all of them—programs like health, education, and the environment. Other times they work separately on projects that affect only their own nation.

Some of the stories you have read about in this book are quite sad. Some stories maybe even made you angry. Some of what has happened to the Indian nations in Wisconsin has been unfair. Native people think that it is important to remember these things so that they don't happen again. But they are looking beyond the past to the future. The Native people are rebuilding their communities. They are trying to improve their schools and create jobs. They are working to clean up the environment and help create healthy places for fish and wildlife. They are trying hard to be modern and give their tribal members the opportunities other Americans have. But the Native people are also trying to stay true to their traditional teachings and cultures.

Think back to the way we started this book. We began with the pow wow, an image that helps us understand the Native experience in Wisconsin. The pow wow circle is filled with many different Indian people, wearing different outfits, and dancing to different songs. But they are celebrating together and sharing their cultures with non-Indians. Like the pow wow, the circle of Indian nations in Wisconsin is still strong. These Native people are celebrating their survival and are excited about their future.

Photo courtesy of Mohican News

Young dancers at a pow wow

148

Glossary

◆ ◆ ◆

access (**ak** ses) Ability to enter or use

algae (**al** jee) Small plants without roots or stems that live in water or on damp surfaces

Algonquian (al **gon** quin) A Native American tribe

alliances (a **li** un ses) Friendly agreements between groups

allies (**al** leyes) Friends, especially during wartime

allotted (uh **lah** ted) To share part of something

Allouez, Jean (ahl oh **way,** jhan) Jesuit priest

ancient (**ayn** chent) Having existed a long time ago

Anishinaabe (ah nih shin **ah** bay) The ancient name for a group formed by the Ojibwe, Odawa, and Potawatomi tribes

annuities (ah **new** uh teez) Yearly payments

archaeologists (ar key **ol** o jists) People who study how people of the past lived based on objects left behind

assimilate (ah **sih** muh late) To make similar or to blend cultures and customs with another

Aw-ke-wain-ze (ah key **wayn** zee) Name of an Ojibwe chief, means "The Old Man"

Aztalan (**az** tuh lan) A village in Wisconsin near Lake Mills

bands (bands) Smaller groups

bison (**bi** sen) Buffalo

Bizhiki (**bee** zhee key) "The Buffalo," a chief of the St. Croix Band

board feet (bord feet) Lumber that is twelve inches long, twelve inches wide, and one inch thick

Bodewadmi (bo deh **wahd** mee) The youngest brother who kept the Sacred Fires lit in a Potawatomi oral tradition

bribery (**bri** buh ree) Gifts offered to people in exchange for favors

Cadotte (cah **dot**) Example of a last name held by early French traders

Cahokia (cah ho kee ah) A city in the Great Lakes area

canneries Factories where foods are canned

casino (ke **see** no) Building where gambling and other entertainment takes place

Cayuga (ki **yu** gah) A Native American tribe

cede (seed) To give up land to another

cerebral palsy (**seh** ruh bruhl **paul** zee) Lack of control over some muscles, caused by brain damage before or during birth

ceremonies (ser uh mo neez) Formal actions, words, or songs that mark an important occasion, such as a wedding or funeral

cession (**seh** shun) The act of giving up one nation's land to another

Champlain, Samuel de (sham **plain**) A Frenchman who established Quebec

Chippewa (chih puh wah) European name for the Ojibwe people

clans (klans) Groups of Native people with a common ancestor

coincidence (co **in** sih dents) Something that happens by chance

commercial fleets (kuh **mer** shuhl fleets) Professional businesses that use fishing boats

commission (cuh **mih** shun) A group of people who meet together to solve a particular problem

confederacy (kuhn **feh** der uh see) Groups (like the Five Nations) that band together for a common purpose

consent (cun **sent**) Agreement

constitutions (**kon** sti **too** shens) Formal written laws and plans of government

Continental Congress (**kon** te nen **tl kong** gris) The government of the American colonies before they adopted the Constitution

converted (ken **vurt** ed) Changing the spiritual beliefs of a group or individuals

Corbine (**cor** bin) Example of a last name held by early French traders

council (**cown** suhl) A governing group

coureurs de bois (coo **rer** deh bwah) French "woods runners"

credit (**kred** it) Time allowed to pay money owed to someone

debts (dets) Amounts of money owed

Denomie (**den** oh mee) Example of a last name held by early French traders

depleted (de **plee** ted) Used up

destitute (**des** tih toot) Lacking enough food, clothing, money, and shelter

droughts (drowts) Long periods of dry weather when little or no rain falls

exercising (**ek** ser **size** ing) Putting into practice, as in exercising the right to vote

effigy (**ef** fih jee) Animal-shaped mounds

Elders (**el** ders) Older people who share wisdom and traditions, and are respected by all people

DRUMS (drums) Determination of Rights and Unity for Menominee Shareholders

gaming dollars (**ga** ming **dol** ers) Money made in the gambling industry, generally from casinos

galena (guh **lee** nah) A grayish lead ore used for making ammunition and paint

Gitchi-Manitoo (**gih** tchee man ih **to**) The Anishinaabe Creator

Gottshall (**got** shawl) A rock shelter located in present day Iowa County

Grignon (gree **noh**) Example of a last name held by early French traders

Haudenosaunee (ho dun a **show** nee) "People of the Long House," name for the confederacy of the Seneca, Cayuga, Onondaga and Mohawk Nations

Hiawatha (hi ah **wah** tha) The Great Peacemaker's interpreter

Hochungra (ho **chun** gruh) Name used by the members of the Ho-Chunk Nation to describe themselves

identity (eye **den** tih tee) Who you are

infantry (**in** fen tree) Foot soldiers

Iroquoian (ear o **qwoy** yun) Of or pertaining to a Native American tribe

Iroquois (**ear** o kwoy) A Native American tribe

isolated (**i** se **la** tid) Kept separated or separate from others

Jesuit (**jehz** wit) Religious order

Ka-be-ma-be (kah bay **mah** bay) "The Wet Month," a chief of the St. Croix Band

Kahnawake (gon ah **wah** gay) An Oneida village

Kiash Matchitiwuk (kee ahsh mah che te wuck) The "Ancient Ones"

Ki-chi-waw-be-sha-shi (kitch chee **wah** bah shosh) "The Great Marten," a leader of the Mole Lake Band

Kickapoo (**kick** ah poo) A Native American tribe

Kish-ki-kaam (**keesh** key kahm) A Potawatomi chief

Lac Courte Oreilles (lac **coo** duh ray) A band of the Ojibwe

Lac du Flambeau (lac du **flam** bo) A band of the Ojibwe

lawsuit (**lah** soot) A case before a court of law that seeks money for damages done to someone

license (**li** sints) Permission or approval from a government

Mackinac (**mak** ih naw) Modern name for Michilimackinac

manoomin (mah **noh** min) Wild rice

Mascouten (mas **coo** ten) A Native American tribe

massacre (**mass** uh ker) A cruel act of killing of innocent people

mature (mut **chure**) Fully grown or developed

Menominee (meh **nah** mih nee) A Native American tribe

Mesquakie (mes **kwaw** kee) A Native American tribe

Metoxin, John (meh **tox** sin) A leader of the Mohicans

Michilimackinac (mish lih **mak** ih naw) Location of a French fort

Midewiwin (mih **day** wih win) Traditional Medicine Lodge religion

Migiizi (meh **gee** zee) A leader of the Mole Lake Band

migrant (**mi** grent) People who move from place to place following available work

migration (mi **gra** shen) Movement from one community to another in the same country

missionaries (**mish** shun air eez) Religious people who try to persuade others to become Christians

missions (**mish** ens) Places of worship where missionaries live and work

Moga Shooch (mo gah **shooch**) Red Banks

Mohican (mo **hee** can) A Native American tribe

Mo-ning-wun-a-kawn-ing (mo ning won a **kaw** ning) "The place of the gold-breasted woodpecker"

motive (**mo** tiv) Reason

Muh-he-con-nuk (mo **he** con nuk) The name the Mohicans give themselves. It means "The People of the Waters That Are Never Still"

Muk-a-day-i-ko-na-yayg (muck a **day** ee ko nah **yayg**) Literally "Black Coats" or Jesuits

Muscoda (**mus** kuh day) City on Wisconsin River

muskellunge (**mus** kuh lunj) Type of fish

negotiators (nih **go** shee ay terz) People who help in making agreements

Neshnabek (neh **shnah** bek) An ancient alliance of Ojibwe, Odawa, and Potawatomi Nations in a Potawatomi oral tradition

neutral (**new** trul) Staying out of disagreement or not taking sides

Nicolet, Jean (nik oh **lay,** jhan) French trader

Odawa (o **dah** wuh) A Native American tribe

Ojibwe (o **jib** way) A Native American tribe

Oneida (o **ny** dah) A Native American tribe

Onondaga (on on **dah** gah) A Native American tribe

Onyoteaka (own yo day a gah) How the Oneida refer to themselves. It means "People of the Standing Stone"

oral tradition (or **el** tre **dish** en) Passing down stories by telling them over and over without writing them down

palisade (pal ih **sade**) A large fence for protection

Paquahwong (pa kwa **wong**) An Ojibwe settlement on the Chippewa river. It means "where the river is wide"

parching (parch ing) Making something very dry by roasting

pelts (pelts) Animal furs that are dried, and sometimes sewed, for trade

Perrot, Nicholas (puh **roh**) French fur trader

persistence (pur **sis** tentz) Refusing to give up on what you want to accomplish

petition (puh **tih** shun) A letter signed by a large number of people requesting that something or someone change

Potawatomi (pah tah **wah** tuh me) A Native American tribe

poverty (**pah** ver tee) Being very poor

prophecies (**prof** eh seez) Predictions about future events

rebellion (re **bel** yun) Armed fight against a government

recognized by the U.S. government (**rek** eg nizd by the U.S. **guv** ern ment) When the tribal government and the U.S. government have a government-to-government relationship

refuge (ref yooj) Protection or shelter from danger or trouble

refugee (**ref** yoo jee) People who are forced by war or disaster to leave their homes

reservations (**rez** er va shens) Areas of land set aside by treaty for tribes to live on

resort (ree **zort**) A place people go for vacations to rest and relax

restore (ri **stor**) To bring something back to its original condition

revealed (ri **veeld**) Showed

royalties (**roy** el tees) Payments, sometimes in the form of taxes

sachems (**sa** chums) Tribal leaders

sacred (**sa** cred) Something deserving of respect

St. Croix (saynt **croy**) A division of the Ojibwe tribe

Sauk (sawk) A Native American tribe

Seneca (**seh** neh kah) A Native American tribe

siblings (**sib** lings) Brothers and sisters

Siouan (soo un) Of or pertaining to a Native American tribe

Sioux (soo) A Native American tribe

Sokaogon (suh **kog** uhn) Mole Lake Ojibwe

sovereign (**sov** ren) As in "sovereign nation," independent; having the right to self-government

sovereignty (**sov** ren tee) Independence

speculators (**speck** yoo la turs) People who try to make money by buying and selling

spiritual (**spir** i choo el) Things that have to do with the soul and spirit

stockade (sto **kade**) A series of high walls to keep out intruders

sustained (se **staind** yeeld **for** eh stree) Provided energy and strength and kept the people going

sustained-yield forestry (se **stained**) An organized plan to replant and regrow trees that are cut down

Tae Kwon Do (tie kwan **do**) A martial art from Korea

Tecumseh (teh **cum** suh) A Shawnee war chief

tension (**ten** shun) Fear and worry

termination (**tur** me **na** shen) The ending of something

treaty (**tree** tee) An official, written agreement between nations

Tuscarora (tus kuh **ror** uh) A nation that joined the Haudenosaunee

valedictorian (val uh dik **tor** e un) The graduating senior with the highest grades in the class

venison (**ven** i sen) Deer

voyageurs (voy uh **jurz**) French-Canadian traders who canoed along the waterways of the Great Lakes and adopted Native foods, medicines, dress, and customs

Waswaagan (wahs **wah** gun) Fire hunters

Werchouski, Katrina (wer **chow** skee) Member of the Ojibwe Nation and a Park Ranger

wigwams (**wig** woms) Traditional homes of Great Lakes Native people made of animal skins or tree bark stretched over bent poles

Winnebago (wih neh **ba** go) A Native American tribe

winnowing (**wih** no wing) To separate chaff by blowing with air

Index

An index is a list of people, places, events, and ideas that you might want to look up and read about. If you do not find the word you are looking for, think of another word that means something like it.

Some words in this index point to other words, such as "Creator. *See* Wisconsin Dells Gitchi-Manitoo." This means that there is another word in the book that means the same thing, but it has a different spelling or name.

Great Lakes Indian Fish and
Wildlife Commission
(GLIFWC), 91–92
Great Law of Peace, the,
112
Great Marten, The, 85-86
Green Bay, 22, 25, 28–29,
50, 54, 98, 119–120, 124,
144

H

Haudenosaunee, the, 112,
116–118
Head Start, 124, 137
Hiawatha, 112
Hochungra, 52
Ho-Chunk Nation, the, *vii*,
16–18, 22, 24–25, 27–31,
38–39, 52–54, 56–58, 60,
62, 64-65, 68, 103, 119
Huron (people), 26, 98,116

I

Indian Removal Act (1830),
103

Indian Reorganization Act
(1934), 44, 87, 107, 121,
135
Indian School of
Milwaukee, the, 110
Iowa, the 54

K

Kahnawake, 117
Kaukauna. *See* Grand
Cackalin
"Keepers of the Fire,"
94–95, 111
Keeshkemun, 80
Keshena, 43, 47–48
Kiash Matchitiwuk, 36
Kickapoo Nation, the, *vii*,
24, 104
Kichiwawbeshashi. *See* The
Great Marten

L

La Crosse, 56
La Follette, Robert M. (U.S.
Senator), 43

La Pointe Band, the. *See*
Ojibwe
Lac Courte Oreilles, the. *See*
Ojibwe
Lac du Flambeau, 43
Lake Champlain, 126
Lake Michigan, 24, 48,
97–98, 102, 104, 119
Lake Superior, 26, 67, 72
Lake Superior Ojibwe, the.
See Ojibwe
Lake Winnebago, 39, 119,
131
Languages
Algonquian, 16–17
Iroquoian, 17
Siouan, 16
Little Elk, 57
Loggers, 41, 82–83
Long House(s), 115, 128
Lost Band (Ojibwe), 87. *See*
Ojibwe
Lutherans, 62

M

Mackinac Island, 28

Madeline Island, 67, 71–72, 74, 82, 87

Main Poc, 101

Manoomin, 67, 70. *See* wild rice

Many Trails Park, 137

Marten Clan, the, 68

Mascouten Nation, the, 24

Medicine Lodge religion, 32

Menominee Nation, the *vii–viii*, 16, 18, 22, 25, 27–30, 34–40, 42–46, 48–49, 68, 119, 133

Menominee Enterprises Incorporated, 46

Menominee Restoration Bill, 47

Menominee Termination Act, 45

Menominee territory, 24, 38

Mesquakie, the *vii*, 16, 24–25, 72

Metoxin, John, 130

Michilimackinac, 28

Midewiwin, 32, 71–72

Migiizi, 86

Miller, Bill, 145

Minocqua, 81

Missionaries 32, 61, 72, 84

Mississippi River, 40, 53–54, 57–58, 103

Missouri Nation(tribe), the, 54

Moga Shooch, 54. *See* Red Banks

Mohawk(s) Nation, the 112, 118, 129

Mohican Nation, the, *vii–viii*, 39, 119

Mohican Nation, Stockbridge-Munsee Band, the, 16–17, 126, 136, 138, 145

Mohican Munsee People, the, 131

Mole Lake (Ojibwe), the. *See* Ojibwe

Moningwunakawning, 67

Montreal, 26

Mound-builders, 13

Muhheconnuk, 126. *See* Mohican

Muscoda, the 65

Muskie, 70

N

National Indian Gaming Act (1988), 48

National Park Service, 142

Neesh (village), 58

Neekoosa, 65

Neshnabek, 94, 111. *See* Anishinaabe

New France, 26. *See* also Canada

Nicolet (Jean), 22, 24, 33, 98

O

Oconto, the 45

Odana, the, 84

Odawa (the middle brother), 94

Odawa Nation, the, 16, 22, 24, 26, 66, 71, 94

Acknowledgements

◆ ◆ ◆

I am grateful to my friends and fellow educators in Indian Country who read portions of this book, corrected errors, and made suggestions. In particular, I'd like to thank the HoCak Wazija Haci Language Division, including Willard Lonetree, Gordon Thunder, and Chloris Lowe Sr. Waewaenen to Alan Caldwell, Dr. Donna Powless, Michelle Dickenson, Sherri LaChapelle, and Geraldine Sanapaw in Menominee Nation. Thanks to Dr. Carol Cornelius and Loretta Metoxen in Oneida and the Stockbridge-Munsee Historical Committee, including Dorothy Davids, Ruth Gudinas, and Bernice Miller Pigeon. I am grateful too to my fellow Anishinabeg: Dana Jackson, Alice Thunder, and Jim Thunder. I appreciate the Native American youth whose short stories are included in the book.

I owe a huge debt to my editor, Bobbie Malone, who kept me on track. Thanks also to Diane Holliday, Kori Oberle, and Bobbie for their help in transforming an adult book into one for students, and to Bobbie and Kori for their fine work on the teacher's guide. Others at the Wisconsin Historical Society that I would like to thank are Jennifer Kolb from the Museum Archaeology program for giving us access to the Wisconsin Indian artifacts in the Society's collections; Erica Schock for obtaining and keeping track of all the graphic elements, and Diane Drexler for managing the project. I am also grateful to Judy Eulberg for her initial photo research, Jill Bremigan for her book design, Amelia Janes for the outstanding maps, Jim Leary from the Folklore department at UW-Madison, and Rick March from the Wisconsin Arts Board for generously allowing us to peruse their slide collections, and everyone who contributed images for the publication.

Miigwech (thank you) to my two sons, Brooks and Dominic, who inspired me to write this book and who remain my toughest reviewers. Finally, Che miigwech to all the boys and girls who honor me by taking the time to read this book.

Manuscript reviewers

Anne Chapman Callaghan
Racine Public Library

Wendy Coyne
Sauk Trails Elementary,
Middleton

Steve D'Onofrio
Sauk Trails Elementary,
Middleton

Vicki Donatell
North Hudson Elementary,
Hudson

Heidi Ebert
West Salem Elementary,
West Salem

Leah Hamann
Eau Claire

Laura Huber
Leopold Elementary,
Madison

J. P. Leary
Consultant, American Indian
Studies Program
Department of Public Instruction

Rick Martinson
West Salem Elementary,
West Salem

Louise Natrop
Retired teacher, Kaukana School
District

Carol Patterson
Tower Rock Elementary,
Prairie du Sac

Lisa Poupart
Chair, American Indian Studies,
University of Wisconsin-Green Bay

Trina Ruyle
Sauk Prairie Middle School,
Sauk Prairie

Fay Stone
Platteville

JoAnn Tiedemann
School Library Media Specialist,
Madison

Tammy Udulutch
Tower Rock Elementary
Prairie du Sac

Marilyn VandeBerg
District Media Coordinator,
Sauk Prairie School District

Classroom reviewers

Dennis Baumann's, Vada Fauver's, and Jeanette Arneson's Fourth Grades
Riverdale Elementary, Muscoda

Jules Cappelle's and Ann DeNure's Fourth and Fifth Grades

Monticello Elementary,
Fourth Grade Students

Indian Community School of
Milwaukee

Susan Freiss' Fourth Grade
Stoner Prairie Elementary,
Verona

Patty Harvey's Fourth Grade
Electa Quinney Elementary,
Kaukana

Marilyn Penn's Fourth Grade
Royal Oaks Elementary,
Sun Prairie

Lisa Stein's Fifth Graders
Lincoln Elementary,
Madison

Roxanne Tibbits' Fourth Grade
Atwater Elementary,
Shorewood